THE CUCKOO'S NEST

THE CUCKOO'S NEST

EXPLORING THE WORLD OF PSYCHOTHERAPY THROUGH FILM

Anoushka Beazley

Registered Offices

John Wiley & Sons, Inc., 111 River Street, Hoboken, NJ 07030, USA

John Wiley & Sons Ltd, New Era House, 8 Oldlands Way, Bognor Regis, West Sussex, PO22 9NQ, UK

For details of our global editorial offices, customer services, and more information about Wiley products visit us at www.wiley.com.

The manufacturer's authorized representative according to the EU General Product Safety Regulation is Wiley-VCH GmbH, Boschstr. 12, 69469 Weinheim, Germany, e-mail: Product_Safety@wiley.com.

Wiley also publishes its books in a variety of electronic formats and by print-on-demand. Some content that appears in standard print versions of this book may not be available in other formats.

Library of Congress Cataloging-in-Publication Data

Names: Beazley, Anoushka author

Title: The cuckoo's nest: exploring the world of psychotherapy through film / Anoushka Beazley.

Description: First edition. | Hoboken, NJ: John Wiley & Sons, Inc, 2026. | Includes bibliographical references and index.

Identifiers: LCCN 2025054223 (print) | LCCN 2025054224 (ebook) | ISBN 9781394334827 paperback | ISBN 9781394334841 adobe pdf | ISBN 9781394334834 epub

Subjects: LCSH: Mental illness in motion pictures

Classification: LCC PN1995.9.M463 B43 2026 (print) | LCC PN1995.9.M463 (ebook)

LC record available at https://lccn.loc.gov/2025054223

LC ebook record available at https://lccn.loc.gov/2025054224

Cover Design: Wiley

Cover Images: © bubaone/Getty Images, © Artrise/Getty Images, © Mariia Iurchenko/Getty Images

Set in 10/12pt Sabon by Straive, Pondicherry, India

For all those who have ever felt not good enough

and

for anyone who has ever experienced loss

Contents

Acknowledgements

The inspiration behind this book began with my own sense of shame. In the early days of my psychotherapy training, I found myself lost and quickly despondent, trying to understand and access the many textbooks and academic papers on the reading lists. What I understood was movies, my undergraduate degree was in Film, and I yearned for characters to explain these psychotherapeutic concepts to me using scripts edited with music. The invitation to write this book for Wiley made my psychotherapy-trainee past self extremely happy but also tapped into a much younger child part of me, a little girl that had written stories from as early as she could write, which always began the same way, 'The girl sat at the window.' This girl had been dreaming, looking out through movies for a way to escape and had no idea then about all the things she would do as a 'grown up' as a way to try and escape her uncomfortable feelings. Thank you, Jake Opie and the Wiley team for first noticing the girl at the window and approaching her book with such wonderful enthusiasm. Thank you to my agent and friend, Rosey Strub, for your steadfastness and girl-boss essence.

Writing compels me, but that does not mean it always does so gently, and in moments where I doubt and I struggle, I have often felt the fear that comes from being ungrounded in this world. Not a strong swimmer, I am both fascinated and fearful of the swirling abysses that dominate our planet. Facing my fear, as I often try to do, I am swimming in the Aegean Sea one day when I look down. The water is crystal clear, and not only have I never swum so close to a school of fish before, but I can see all too clearly how the seabed has suddenly both widened and deepened beneath me and I am swimming in a valley! I feel my breath vanish, then become shallow, waves of panic arrive, the last thing you want underwater. It's scary! The same feeling I have being caught unawares in a sea valley, I can also have at other times in my life, even in the writing of a book. I am now above water, writing these acknowledgements, hoping this book will help some of you find your way out of the abyss.

Thank you to Maha Khan Phillips and Noelle Britton for the various contributions offered in the writing of this book. Thank you to Lyn Latreille for formatting the book, a generous and sensitive soul who I am grateful to have on speed dial. Thank you, Bernhard Hilbert, for opening my eyes to the quest of the cuckoo.

I am happy to be able to thank my supervisor, Cholena Mountain, not only for her Nurturing Parent energy during my training but also for her unwavering support of me when I was looking for a home for the book. Thank you, Adrienne Lee, Director at The Berne Institute – my Transactional Analysis home for three years, for your vision and for seeing me with it. Over the course of my life I have had many wonderful therapists who have all played a part in the concretising of this book: Maureen Brown, a Wiccan high priestess and psychotherapist who modelled self-love and feminine power; Deborah Sless, my first introduction to an authoritarian presence in my life who advocated for my autonomy, William Cornell, a veritable alchemist whose wisdom and kindness turned anger into love; Geraldine Healy, proof that when I call for a good witch, something good this way comes and Pamela Lanigan, tied to no official institution, academic or otherwise, a modern-day witch who worshipped the unconscious and the unbound.

Thank you to my trifecta of angelic image illustrators, Ariella Beazley, Mia Beazley and Alabama Beazley who drew my first diagrams for the book. Thank you for choosing me to be your mother. Whatever happens, let's just make sure we talk about it, cry about it and then laugh about it, in that order.

Thank you Max for being the John Rose to my Moira Rose.

And finally, to every single person who has ever been involved in the creation of a film or television series – thank you for making a little space in a complicated world where people can go to heal.

What you did was impulsive, capricious, and melodramatic. . . but it was also wrong.

Moira Rose – *Schitt's Creek*

Foreword

Through the pages of this fascinating book, *The Cuckoo's Nest: Exploring the World of Psychotherapy through Film*, Anoushka Beazley invites us to explore the mysterious challenges of being human. In her own words, '*The human experience is, up to this point at least, characterised by shame and loss. This book has been conceived and written, with love, in the hope of helping to better understand who we are underneath all the layers of "stuff" that we carry.*'

The 'stuff we carry' has been an abiding and humane focus of transactional analysis and related models of psychotherapy within the humanistic tradition since the 1960s.

The novel *One Flew Over the Cuckoo's Nest*, written by Ken Kesey in 1962, explored themes of individuality, pain and pride, sanity and madness, and the struggle against institutional power. It became a countercultural symbol, critiquing societal conformity and the dehumanising effects of medical and psychiatric authority. The novel was later popularised by an extremely successful film starring Jack Nicholson. Here, drawing upon other classic movies, Anoushka illustrates and humanises the challenges of being human in a world that can at times seem quite mad.

In 1964, *Games People Play* by Eric Berne became an international bestseller. Berne had been developing a new approach to psychotherapy, which he called transactional analysis, and he first described it in two professional books to introduce the concepts of TA to his colleagues. *GPP* was aimed at a broader audience, as Berne stressed the need for psychotherapy to use words that ordinary people could understand and relate to. He succeeded with *GPP* which, rather unexpectedly, became an international bestseller. Berne's book gave people a new way, in a humorous and often ironic voice, of thinking about how and why people got along – or, more to the point, didn't get along so very well. Like *One Flew Over the Cuckoo's Nest*, it hit a nerve and opened people's eyes.

GPP was followed by a number of other so-called 'pop psychology' books, those in the self-help realm. Over the decades, transactional analysis has had an unusual publishing history. On the one hand, there have been a variety of books that represent the pop psychology, self-help genre, drawing upon the aspects of the ideas and language of TA that are very accessible, useful and meaningful to people. These are books that help people think about themselves, their relationships and the hopes and frustrations they experienced in their lives.

At the same time, transactional analysis has continued to develop as a serious methodology of psychotherapy, counselling, educational strategies and organisational management. Sixty years on, since *GPP*, there has also been a second genre of TA books aimed at professional audiences that has continued to evolve and deepen both the theory and the techniques of transactional analysis.

Anoushka's book weaves those two strands together, accomplishing two tasks: the first in keeping with the 'user-friendly' heritage of TA, she has written a book that is accessible, readable and highly engaging – readers will find themselves, family and friends captured in the pages of this book. It provides a hands-on, useful overview and application of the theory of transactional analysis, with each chapter concluding with questions that invite self-reflection. At the same time, the chapters in this book convey all the basic elements of TA theory with a depth and insight that will appeal to lay and professional readers alike.

One of the important steps in the evolution of TA was the development of what came to be called the TA 101, the basic seminar that contains all of the fundamental TA theory. It is taught all around the world. While it is common for people to take the TA 101 to learn about themselves, the TA 101 is the first step in pursuing further professional training. In this book, Anoushka takes the TA 101 to the movies in a unique and very creative way. She explores the central ideas of transactional analysis, taking them up with depth and bringing them alive through the stories and images of classic cinema.

The movies Anoushka draws upon capture the human psyche. These are the movies that convey the hopes, the fears, the pain and the triumphs of the human spirit, movies filled with wizards, witches, ogres, mermaids, fantasy, deceits, tragedies and truths. What is it about these movies? Why do certain movies become classics? Why are there certain movies that people return to over and over again? Anoushka has drawn upon these classics. These are the movies that touch us. These are the movies alive with creativity, intensity, drama and humour that speak to aspects of life that challenge us all. These are movies that provide an emotional catharsis, psychological recognition and opportunities for identification, recognition that '*I'm not alone in these things that I struggle with.*' Movies have a way of giving us an opportunity to see something about ourselves, to feel something about ourselves. They are also a form of entertainment, and in that, they can be an avenue of escape. But here Anoushka invites us to slow down, to look again, to look *in* and to reflect on ourselves.

She takes up the themes, the familiarity, the stories, the drama, the hopes of these movies and then links them, not simply to ideas from transactional analysis, but to the work we all do as psychotherapists and the work patients do in psychotherapy. It is hard work.

But she doesn't just sit with us in a movie theatre; she also invites us into her own life. Part of what makes this book so alive and compelling is that, along with her discussions of these classic movies, she intertwines it with stories and struggles from her own life, her training as a psychotherapist, which is not always an easy process, and aspects of her family and family history that are woven deeply into the woman she is and the therapist she is.

The warp and weft that Anoushka weaves together in these pages create a unique, compelling and compassionate book – one that I am sure Eric Berne would have greeted with respect and delight.

William F. Cornell, M.A., TSTA-P
Pittsburgh, Pennsylvania, USA
27 September 2025

Prologue

I grew up watching movies. A friend of my father's owned a video shop and I would bunk off school to watch movies like *The Godfather*, *The Texas Chainsaw Massacre* and *Endless Love*, movies which at 13 I probably shouldn't have been watching. Movies helped me to live and I didn't even know it. I lost myself in the colours, the pictures, the music. The characters were so mesmerising, so inspirational, so brave. I was transported to other worlds, and I had no idea as a child that this made it a little easier to be in the world I lived in. Horror movies with their blood and gore and me and my popcorn, hiding. Gangster movies with their guns and bullets, and me on the edge of my seat, surviving. Romance movies with their impossible love and happy endings and me, heart beating, hoping.

True Romance had blood, guns and love, as well as Alabama Worley. Her beauty was her vulnerability and valour, epitomising two important qualities you need in this world. We will battle, we will fall, we will bruise. And then we get up to lament, to laugh, to love. But as I've gotten older, it's become imperative to admit that I don't always know how to do that. That it isn't always obvious. That what is easy to others might not be easy for me. And that sometimes I might need a little help

Have I always known I wanted to be a psychotherapist? No. When I was younger, I wanted to be two things. The first was a pathologist. A childlike logic in wanting to look inside the dead to understand better how to live a life. The second – an archaeologist. It seemed essential to excavate, and that by learning about the past we could better understand the present. That's what made me want to write this book and hoped it would be something. Alabama might find helpful. I saw myself in her and in many other characters in this book because that's what movies do – they help us learn about each other and ourselves. This is the book I wish I'd had when I was training to be a psychotherapist. It is also the book I wish I'd had as a teenager. Read it in chronological order or when a film or theory resonates with your life. My choice of films was spontaneous and will hopefully stimulate some of you into a new state of awareness. Fusing psychotherapy and film, I bring you these experiences and this book from a place of deep intimacy. May this book bring you a touch of clarity in the stormy art of living.

> *Amid the chaos of that day, when all I could hear was the thunder of gunshots and all I could smell was the violence in the air, I look back and am amazed that my thoughts were so clear and true, that three words went through my mind endlessly, repeating themselves like a broken record. 'You're so cool. You're so cool. You're so cool.'*
>
> Alabama Worley – *True Romance*

1

The Parent, Adult and Child Model and *Inside Out*

Theory: Parent, Adult and Child Model

A psychological theory from transactional analysis (Berne 1961) introduces the idea of internal Parent, Adult and Child parts of us which develop as children and contribute to forming our personality, informing how we behave and interact with others for the rest of our lives.

Movie: *Inside Out (2015)*

Riley must leave all her friends in school and the life she knows after her dad gets a new job and she moves to San Francisco with her parents. She tries to go with the flow but it's not easy and the move creates stress which leads to Riley feeling overwhelmed. In the movie, Riley's emotions are represented as people who are part of Riley's personality and are responsible for operating a console in the headquarters of Riley's mind, the place where decisions about important matters are made. When overwhelm turns to chaos, Riley's behaviour and relationships become adversely affected and mayhem ensues in headquarters. The movie explores emotions, their purpose and impact, through the story of a little girl trying hard to cope with monumental changes in her life.

What We're Doing

In this chapter, we will be looking at the Parent, Adult and Child model through the eyes of 11-year-old Riley, the main character in *Inside Out*. As we learn about the model, we will use it to understand and explore Riley's relationship to her emotions. Using my own experience in training, I invite you to consider how the theory may relate to your life.

In a backwards timeshift, Riley's parents cast their eyes on their baby girl as she comes into the world for the first time. The wondrousness of this tiny, amazing being has them enveloped in an overflowing love. The love they feel allows for the creation of 'Joy.' And this is how we first meet her – Joy – one of Riley's emotions living inside her body. '*Just me and Riley forever,*' murmurs Joy. Joy sees herself as a leader, which makes sense as she has the peppy spirit and smile of a cheerleader, bouncy and ready for action. When Joy meets Riley for the first time, her heart explodes with happiness. She is bathed in love. She radiates with golden light as she operates the console in the headquarters of Riley's mind, happily narrating the story of Riley's life so far. Joy takes Riley's first-ever happy memory of Riley and her parents in the hospital, a core memory in the shape of a ball and puts this precious core memory ball safely away to preserve it forever. And so Riley's library of core memories begins to form; so far, each memory is joyful. The emotions, like joy, that form from these core memories can be found in the Parent, Adult or Child ego states. (Don't worry, we'll get to what that means!)

Joy was happy thinking of herself as Riley's only emotion, which was understandable as she was, for 33 seconds, the only one. However, to Joy's surprise, Riley's newborn baby's cry heralds another emotion, Sadness – a slouched, shuffling, sorrowful, blue-coloured little girl – who suddenly appears beside Joy at the console. This is a huge shock to Joy. She thought she was the only emotion in Riley's body and definitely the only one with any influence on Riley, but Sadness is able to make Riley cry, very loudly. Sadness confuses Joy, '*I'm not actually sure what she does but I've checked and there's nowhere for her to go,*' says Joy about Sadness. When Joy sees how Sadness has the ability to change what Riley is feeling from happy to sad, she says, '*I just want to fix that.*' We get an idea of how Joy feels about Sadness which in reality is how the sadness part of ourselves is often perceived. Sadness can also be found in the Parent, Adult or Child ego states.

In the world of Riley's mind, Sadness walks slowly in her round body. '*Crying helps me slow down and obsess over the weight of life's problems,*' is how she describes herself. After Sadness, Joy quickly meets a whole gang of emotions who arrive to take up space right next to her and suddenly, there's not a whole lot of room in headquarters. There's the thin, timid, constantly vigilant guy called Fear. There's the sassy, sarcastic, fashionista girl – Disgust. And there's the stocky, fiery, hot-headed man – Anger – who checks to make sure things are fair. Fear, disgust and anger can also all be found in the Parent, Adult or Child ego states.

In the present day, Joy organises specific tasks for the other emotions to help prepare Riley for her first day at her new school. She asks Fear to compile a list of all the things that can possibly go wrong. She asks Disgust to keep Riley from being '*poisoned physically and socially.*'

And Riley wasn't the only one starting a new school. It was my first day of a two-year diploma course in Transactional Analysis counselling. Autumn, a fresh September morning. A crisp wind whistling ever so softly through the trees. I feel my legs slow as my destination comes into view, edges and colours of a building becoming clearer. Ivy trails over the bricks and I follow the vine to the ground. What am I doing here, outside this pretty detached Victorian house in a leafy London suburb? Suddenly, I'm not sure if I know. What is this feeling? Am I scared? First day of school? Hardly. I'm a grown woman. School was a long time ago.

I may not know what I am doing here but I do know what brought me here. Sadness. After my father passed away, a surprisingly cataclysmic event in my life, the crying did not stop. Eventually, I felt that if I was crying every day anyway, I should be somewhere where emotional expression felt germane to the subject at hand.

Riley's dad gets a call to go to work and leaves. Sadness says: '*Dad just left us. He doesn't love us anymore. That's sad.*' Sitting here, I think back to when my dad died and the emotion I felt was the same as Riley – sadness.

The format of my course was one weekend a month, and I remember thinking no problem! Little did I know how much I would come to dread Saturday by the time Friday evening rolled around. To be clear, it's not as if I was sacrificing anything dear to me on those particular weekends, and yet now, the idea of having two days sat in one room, 16 hours and 18 strangers, made me regret not having previously engaged in anything passionately and regularly enough to ensure my weekends would be too precious to give up. My first day of this new learning was about to teach me my first psychological theory, which would not only help me understand how Riley and I were feeling on our first day of school but also shed light on all the human interactions I had ever had in my life!

It all begins with the Parent, the Adult and the Child (always capitalised), says our tutor Bella. She drew three circles one on top of the other. She called them ego states (Figure 1.1). Bella talks to us, a group of tentative therapists in training as we choose our seats on comfy chairs and two-seater sofas. Bella occupies a central position, cementing her authority at the top of the room. She emanates a maternal kindness, a warmth. Oh, the joy! Joy is an emotion that can be felt in the gaze of a caring and nurturing parent, and that is the kind of joy portrayed by the character Joy in *Inside Out*. And as Bella starts talking, my eyes water. She'd barely written her name on the board and told us where the fire exits were. What was happening to me? Riley and I experienced similar beginnings at our new schools (Fig. 1.1).

The Parent ego state is made up of information and messages accumulated from Riley's parents, parental-type figures, other family members, teachers and bosses.

The Adult ego state is made up of momentary decision-making processes in the present.

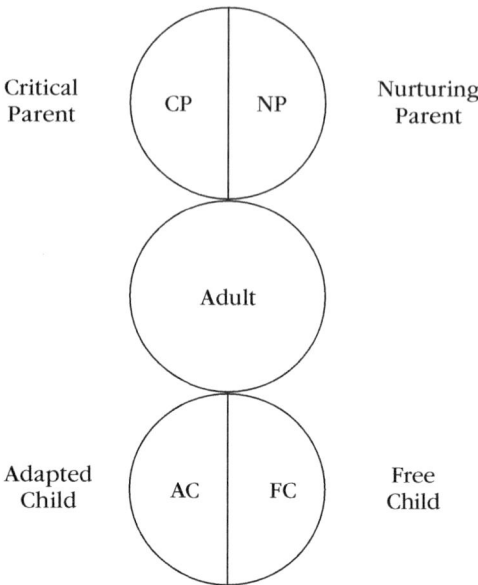

Fig. 1.1 The Parent, Adult and Child Model of Ego States. Source: Berne (1961) / with permission of American Psychological Association

The Child ego state is made up of emotional and somatic experiences and memories, like the sadness Riley feels about missing her old school.

As Riley stands in her new class introducing herself, Joy selects a core memory ball from Riley's conveyor belt of core memories to help her tell her story. The memory is a snowy day in Minnesota on the rink with mum and dad. But as Riley starts talking about the fun she had in her old life, Sadness touches the memory ball and turns a gold-coloured core memory ball, blue. Riley starts to cry – she misses her old life. As my tutor Bella speaks, I wonder if I'd like to cry at that moment, though I'm not entirely sure what about. Riley and I are experiencing similar beginnings at our new school but in front of all these strange adults, I do not cry.

Bella starts to speak about parents and asks if any of us would like to say how the subject of parents makes us feel. A hot torrent of unease swirls in my stomach. I'm terrified of opening my mouth, of being judged or laughed at and yet strangely, I am just as terrified of not opening my mouth. That feels weird. Damned if I do and damned if I don't.

Riley was also feeling so many different feelings in her new school. As her teacher spoke, she didn't know which one of her emotions to listen to first. But what she did know was that they were all talking at once.

A little voice in my head says, '*You can do it – Bella said she wants to hear from people.*' I think '*Well, ok then,*' until another voice pipes up, '*Wait a minute, she said people. How do you know that applies to you?*' Thoughts in my head jump into numbered cars and suddenly my mind transforms into a racetrack, each thought driving their own car, the sound of a loud hum as my brain whizzes really fast. '*Just be quiet,*' says the thought driver of one car, dismissively. '*Go on, tell her the stuff you want to say,*' says another, encouragingly. '*You've missed your chance now,*' says a new voice, knowingly. '*It'll be awful if you speak at the same time as someone else,*' says another fearfully.

I'm not sure which race car furiously careened off the track first, making all the other cars collide into a pile-up, but suddenly I opened my mouth to speak, and when I had finished, the loud hum had stopped. Wide eyes and blank expressions stare back at me. I don't know these people yet, their resting faces, their tells. I feel my brown skin flush red. I need an antiseptic for my hive-like panic of being seen, currently spreading across my body. Bella seems clueless to my predicament. Why is that? Could it be that what I feel, which I firmly believe is flashing neon and entirely obvious to the world, is not as obvious as I think?

Riley starts becoming overwhelmed by her emotions and all the thoughts she hears coming from each one of them. Joy panics. Disgust notices the cool kids whispering as Riley clams up and doesn't know what to say, whilst Fear exclaims, '*Did you see their face?! They're judging us!!!*' Riley sees the kids whispering and feels scared. She begins to cry, and crying at her new school on her first day in front of the class forms a new blue-coloured core memory, which is sad. Joy has never seen a blue-coloured core memory as it is formed. She assumed all Riley's core memories, the fundamentally important ones, were gold and happy. Listening to Riley cry, Joy becomes agitated, and in an attempt to fix what she believes to be an emotional catastrophe, she tries to get rid of the core memory, to get rid of the sadness. Sadness cries out, pleading for Joy to stop. Joy and Sadness tussle, and in the chaos, all Riley's core memory balls scatter into the deep recesses of Riley's mind.

Riley's core memories are linked to different aspects of her personality referred to in the movie as islands. She has family island, honesty island, friendship island and it is these, and all the other islands together, that make Riley who she is. But with the core memories lost, Riley's 'personality islands' become untethered. Joy and Sadness are yanked into the swirling abyss of Riley's unconscious, their frightened shrieks echoing as headquarters is plunged into confusion. The girls leave an even more petrified than usual Fear, a shell-shocked Anger and an unimpressed Disgust all alone to regulate the decision-making headquarters of Riley's day-to-day life. The parts of Riley's personality that are powered by the core memories are no longer functioning and, without Joy running headquarters, Riley cannot be happy.

Both Riley and I feel our emotions from the past which inform how we feel in the present and will impact how we behave in the future. Joy, who loves Riley dearly, only knows one way to help her and that is to force her to be happy. Sadness, who loves Riley dearly, isn't so sure, but she's too sad to know why she's not sure or construct a compelling argument. Disgust, who loves Riley dearly, wants to protect Riley and keep her safe, so she sends her perceived messages about what people are thinking about her in order to keep her separate from them – but they might not all be true. And Anger, who loves Riley dearly, feels something has got to change, things are unfair and he'd like to explode.

Bella said that we each have a Parent inside of us. She called this Parent part an ego state. This is not a real parent but an idea of a parent – an internalised parent-like concept that we create ourselves based on messages given to us growing up, verbally and non-verbally from our caregivers. This information could be from our own parents as well as an assortment of parent-type figures: teachers, aunts and uncles, bosses, grandparents, friends of parents and older siblings. These messages help form our core beliefs, beliefs which make us feel good and bad and something in between.

Bella drew a vertical line down the centre of the top circle. On one side, she wrote Critical Parent and on the other side of the line, Nurturing Parent. In a simple example, Bella says the Critical Parent part might pay close attention to how the child crosses the road. Once the child is safely on the other side of that road, the Nurturing Parent might take over and in a less critical manner take an interest in the child's day – enquiring, advising and wishing them good luck on their test. Later on, as we grow up and into adulthood, our internalised Critical Parent kicks in at every busy road and we take a step away from fast traffic onto the safer pavement, without even thinking, unconsciously. We go for an interview and are able to wish ourselves well; an internalised Nurturing Parent voice has become second nature.

The Nurturing Parent could also instruct the child in crossing the road just like the Critical Parent could also advise on the test and they'd both have a different way of doing it, equally valuable. It's about how it's done, and how it's done dictates the kinds of core memories we form.

For example, what happens if the Critical Parent gets overly critical crossing the road or talking about a test? If someone shouts at us at the side of the road or about our test, how does that make us feel? What message do we internalise about that moment or future moments similar to that one? Similarly, what happens if the Nurturing Parent is overly nurturing – for instance, by being overly intrusive or engulfing? If the parent does the homework for the child, and the child never learns for themselves. The nurturing parent can become damaging in its own way. What if there is an absence of a Critical Parent and/or Nurturing Parent? Maybe the child goes to school without being given the books they need? What if no one even knows there is a child crossing a road or a test to be taken? The word we know as nurture originates from the Latin word 'nutrire' which means 'to suckle' or 'to nourish.' How have we been nourished and how do we now go on to nourish ourselves?

With the help of Bella, and just like Riley, I'm starting to learn how our personality can be shaped and affected depending on our core memories, and how the beliefs we form about ourselves and our environment are influenced by our early experiences and relationships. We need both Parent parts for different things and ideally we need them to function in a state of balance. This creates a state of calm equilibrium for the child. It is from this solid foundation that the child learns to cope with distress. Riley has to cope with the stress of leaving friends behind and moving to San Francisco but by Joy trying her best to control Sadness, Riley has no way to express how she feels. Sadness is a biological and normal response to a sad event involving grief and loss.

As I watched Riley navigate her emotions, I started to think about how perfectly the movie illustrates how these states become formed when we are very young, sometimes too young to even speak and that right now I might be experiencing Bella as a Nurturing Parent by a very young part of me. It was as if her face came right up close next to mine the way you do with a baby. Fine auburn wisps framed a smile that felt just for me, like Riley's Joy! A tidal wave of embarrassment washes over my hot cheeks as I can feel how much I want this teacher, who I have just met, to notice me, to see the good in me and to think well of me. Discovering that I have a much stronger Critical Parent than Nurturing Parent puts me in touch with my sadness. My Child ego state was activated as I got in touch with old yet familiar feelings. What had I been expecting?

Exercises

1. Think of what your internalised Parent might look like. What emotions do you feel when it speaks to you? How do you remember experiencing your parents when you were growing up?
2. What does your Critical Parent say in your head? Which emotions do you feel when it speaks to you? What are examples of a Critical Parent from your childhood?
3. What does your Nurturing Parent say? Which emotions do you feel when it speaks to you? What are examples of a Nurturing Parent from your childhood?

Reference

Berne, E. (1961). *Transactional Analysis in Psychotherapy: A Systematic Individual and Social Psychiatry*. New York: Grove Press.

2

The Parent, Adult and Child Model and *Inside Out*

Theory: Parent, Adult and Child Model

A psychological theory from transactional analysis (Berne 1961) introduces the idea of internal Parent, Adult and Child parts of us which develop as children and contribute to forming our personality, informing how we behave and interact with others for the rest of our lives.

Movie: *Inside Out (2015)*

Riley must leave all her friends in school and the life she knows after her dad gets a new job and she moves to San Francisco with her parents. She tries to go with the flow but it's not easy and the move creates stress which leads to Riley feeling overwhelmed. In the movie, Riley's emotions are represented as people who are part of Riley's personality and are responsible for operating a console in the headquarters of Riley's mind, the place where decisions about important matters are made. When overwhelm turns to chaos, Riley's behaviour and relationships become adversely affected and mayhem ensues in headquarters. The movie explores emotions, their purpose and impact, through the story of a little girl trying hard to cope with monumental changes in her life.

What We're Doing

In this chapter, we will be looking at the Parent, Adult and Child model through the eyes of 11-year-old Riley, the main character in *Inside Out*. As we learn about the model, we will use it to understand and explore Riley's relationship to her emotions. Using my own experience in training, I invite you to consider how the theory may relate to your life.

Here we are. Second day of the first weekend of my training course, a day commonly known as 'Sunday' but currently being renamed in my head as *'Are You Sure You Want To Do This?'* People walk in with a slightly heavier gait, noticeably less enthusiastic than yesterday – it definitely looked like everyone had their own 'stuff' going on. The reason? Can't say for sure but the top contender appears to be that for homework we were all asked to reflect on our ego states and this brought uncomfortable emotions to the surface. We were asked to think about all the messages that make up our Critical Parent and our Nurturing Parent – and when we might have heard them in our childhood. It is impossible to ignore the sombre mood in the room.

Though it feels like our homework might have allowed us to access younger feelings, Bella points to the middle one of three stacked circles in the PAC model – the Adult ego state. The Adult is responsible for making decisions in real time, in a logical manner without too much emotional thought – I bought my train ticket in my Adult ego state. It is a more objective place, more rational and thoughtful in processing and evaluating situations. A place to observe from a more detached and unemotional viewpoint. Despite being an adult, now being asked to give it some real thought, I wasn't sure how completely Adult I always felt. Often, I would be speaking from my adult body but I was slowly realising that there might also be the voice of the Critical Parent somewhere in there, and at other times, maybe also the Child. It made sense why sometimes I felt like my mind's headquarters was as crowded as Riley's.

I had no idea at that point the depth of the emotional process I was to embark on. I now knew that being bullied in school had formed a core memory, blue and sad, and I wondered about all the others. Seeing Riley and all her emotions in her new school showed me how the different parts of us – memories, feelings, thoughts – impacted how we felt and behaved in different aspects of our current lives. And there was still the rest of Sunday to go.

Along with a Parent ego state and an Adult ego state, we each also have a Child ego state inside of us – Bella points to the bottom circle. She divides the Child circle into Adapted Child and Free Child (Fig. 1.1). This part is made up of emotions that have been felt by the child and internalised. The Adapted Child is the part of the child who has had to emotionally adapt. In adapting, they have had to put their own needs aside to meet the needs of others. They have learned to bury their feelings in the hope of better tolerating their environment. When Riley suppresses her sadness because her mother asks her to be happy about the new move, the opposite of what Riley is feeling, she is adapting. When she sits alone eating her lunch in the playground, she tries to hide her sadness, scared of what people will think of her. Again, she is adapting.

During the hunt to find Riley's lost core memories, Joy and Sadness meet Bing Bong, an old imaginary friend Riley created in her even younger years. He slumps to the floor devastated, sad he has lost his toy rocket. Joy says with a big smile, '*we can fix this*.' She makes funny faces, tickles him to try and make him laugh. Sadness approaches Bing Bong in a different way. '*I'm sorry they took your rocket. They took something that you loved. It's gone forever.*' By naming it and acknowledging it, Sadness recognises Bing Bong is hurting and sits beside him in his sadness.

The Free Child is the part that feels comfortable to be emotionally and behaviourally free. To be themselves and do and say what they want and not worry about the consequences. And just like the Critical and Nurturing Parent, we also need both parts of the Child. We need the Free Child to be able to play, be spontaneous and feel joy. We also need the Adapted Child to listen, to sit patiently in the classroom so we can learn how to read and write. But what if one part of our Child dominates or speaks out at the wrong time? What if the Free Child doesn't get formed at all?

I look around the room, starting to realise we are all made up of so many different parts. I smile at the girl sitting opposite me. She makes a funny face and I let out a little chuckle. Bella says, '*Hello, Free Child, nice to have you with us.*'

The circles in Fig. 1.1 are separate, the boundaries between them clearly defined. Such separation illustrates an understanding that we are consciously aware of the part of us reacting in any given situation. This is not the norm!

Bella has started to write words up on the whiteboard. Words that describe how any one of our ego states might be feeling at any given moment. One stands out – shame. It was now clear in no uncertain terms that, despite a successful interview and a brand-new A4 notebook on my lap, I'm not sure what I'm doing here. I am overwhelmed, my heart beating faster. I feel uncomfortable with everyone's eyes upon me. I was grateful to see that Bella had lost none of the warmth in her eyes after hearing my class contribution. She even thanked me for being the first to talk and illustrate the Parent, Adult and Child model.

Bella broke down what I said:

Critical Parent: *Nobody wants to hear what you have to say.*
Adult: *I'm here right now so I will speak.*
Adapted Child: *I feel scared. I don't want to be hurt.*

Remembering some of my core memories, I can see myself at school, knowing the answer to a teacher's question but being too frightened to speak. As school progressed and the bullying increased, I learnt how not to be seen. And like Riley, I didn't want anyone to see my sadness. I felt it might make things worse. I look around the room at my new classmates, all these years later, no longer a little girl, and wonder if the thoughts driving around in the racing cars of my mind have come from the emotions I had felt and repressed at school. Even though school was a long time ago, maybe those painful emotions were still with me. As we started to share our stories, it appeared I was not the only one in my class discovering emotions belonging to my Parent, Adult and Child parts.

'*Any questions?*' asks Bella. I do have one, but I dare not ask. Where is my Nurturing Parent? It occurs to me that though these parts have been created in the past and are historic, they are also alive, immediate and constantly being added to and reshaped.

Riley is told that this is going to be good for them. A new city and a new school, and it's going to be fun. Riley puts on her bag and a smile for her parents and her first day at school. Riley misses her old friends and gets sad and cries when she thinks about them and the fact that she doesn't have any new ones. She gets angry about having to be in a new school, shouts at and lies to her parents.

The circles in Fig. 1.1 are an ideal example of the human intrapsychic process. It is much more common that we experience the overlapping of the ego states as in Fig. 2.1 where there is a sense of not always knowing which part of us is speaking or feeling. A feeling of being out of control, not being able to access the part we wish to speak from or not knowing how to stop a part of us speaking. In other words, feeling like we are acting from our Adult ego state but being unconsciously influenced by the Parent or the Child ego state.

The Parent ego state can encroach onto the Adult ego state and reduce the part of us that is able to make logical decisions. The diminished Adult ego state becomes affected by messages from the Parent ego state. The

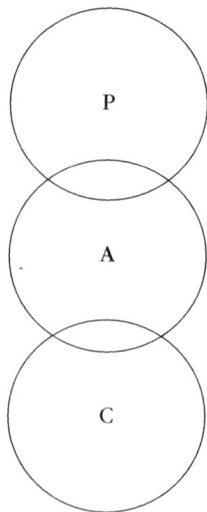

Fig. 2.1 The Parent, Adult and Child Model of Ego States

Child ego state can overlap the Adult ego state, filling up the Adult space with emotions and somatic (body-felt) experiences from the Child.

The degree of overlap between the circles (Fig. 2.1) will differ from person to person. The more overlap between Riley's ego states, the less awareness she has of which part of her is operating at any given time. Fear, Disgust and Anger were making all the decisions in headquarters and without Joy, Riley's parents couldn't recognise Riley's behaviour at all. Riley's Mum had told her to be happy about the move and with Joy being in charge, Riley's Parent ego state received the message '*we have to be happy*.' With Joy out of headquarters, there were different messages.

Joy says, '*nothing bad can happen while she's sleeping*.' Bella explains that sleeping can be a sign of depression because, like Joy, clients also believe nothing bad can happen if they're not awake. Growing up, I remember my mother would have terrible migraines and sleep for hours whilst my father would sleep off a daily hangover for hours. The relationship between the physical body and emotional body seemed obvious to me then but I didn't have the words to explain their connection. However, as a child, I internalised the sadness in my Child ego state and it just sat there, unacknowledged and unprocessed feelings, becoming part of how I interacted with the world.

The film shows how Riley's parents also have their own emotional confusion inside them, just as everybody does. Riley's understanding of the world is in part influenced by the way the emotional control centres operate for her parental caregivers; her earliest and most important influences. The idea of core memories is a feature of ego state theory, suggesting that our very first experiences, our core memories, stimulate emotional responses which we then go on to classify and internalise as part of us. Messages and instructional information are filed into the Parent ego state and emotional experiences, also known as somatic experiences, form the Child ego state. How we choose to emotionally classify the information and experiences will depend on many factors including personality, environment and early parental influences. As children, we often tend to classify experiences according to what makes us feel good or what makes us feel bad. Life is seen as binary in order to be understood by our developing brains. Only when we grow up, and often in therapy, do we recognise the need to reclassify our experiences and process the emotions that hold us stuck in our core self-limiting beliefs as we learn about conflicting feelings, for example, loving my parents but also feeling sad around them, angry towards them and scared of them.

Back at headquarters, Anger is furious and also too angry to know how to do anything! He is angry that the last time he can remember Riley being happy was when they were still living in Minnesota. He makes an executive decision to run away. As Riley steals money from her Mum's purse, we see 'honesty island' give a loud rumble, a sudden shake and eventually collapse under its own weight, falling dramatically into the abyss.

Meanwhile, Joy and Sadness find Riley's lost core memories and are trying their hardest to get back to headquarters to stop Riley from running away. Joy snaps at Sadness, admonishing her for making Bing Bong, Riley's imaginary friend, feel worse than he already does by talking about his sadness. Sadness, thankfully, ignores her and after Bing Bong cries and has a cathartic release, he feels better. Joy is genuinely shocked and asks Sadness how she did that. '*I don't know, he was sad, so I listened,*' answers Sadness, oblivious to her own wondrous ability to be just as sad as she feels. Joy was convinced that the core memory Sadness touched was a happy memory. Joy's entire world view is rocked when she discovers that the only reason the memory was classified as joy was because of the love and hugs that arrived after the sadness came, the sadness Riley had felt when she lost her hockey game. Joy sees that without Sadness, there would have been no core memory at all.

I wonder if Riley's core memory should be reclassified 'Joy/Sadness.' It takes the near breaking of Riley's personality islands and the near loss of her core memories for Joy to fully comprehend the vital role that Sadness plays in Riley's life. It reminds me that sometimes we need to collapse, to break down and feel so lost before we can start to find ourselves again. Joy relinquishes her control over the control panel at headquarters, handing it over to Sadness to do what she feels is best for Riley, but Riley needs them both. Joy offers Sadness a collection of core memories for her to touch and reclassify and as she does this Riley starts to sob and tell her parents how unhappy she is away from her friends. As Riley gives herself permission to feel her Sadness, she starts to feel better. Her personality islands come back to life. Later, her mind is revamped with a brand-new console and a whole load of new buttons to press, like Puberty (*Inside Out 2!*). Anger sees that he has access to the '*entire curse word library.*' As we grow, our emotional systems become more sophisticated, like computer software, they get new emotional software updates.

The movie and our main girl Riley gave us a first-time look at how emotions live inside our bodies. Seeing Riley's emotions manifest as cute little people showed us exactly how our own emotions show up outside of our bodies and into our daily lives. Reducing the contamination/overlap between ego states involves developing a deeper awareness of what we are feeling and who we are. Once Riley began to eliminate the confusion of what was happening in her mind and body, she understood herself better. In many ways, Joy has controlled Sadness since she was little, believing that Sadness had no function and needed to be managed/buried. Joy contributed to both unhealthy and limiting Critical Parent messages as well as healthy and secure Nurturing Parent messages in Riley's Parent ego state. She learned to do that from observing Riley's parents, from what she sees in the world around her and from aspects of Riley's own personality.

It can be confusing for a child to understand all the messages and feelings they receive. This is why, as adults, we sometimes get to a certain point in our lives where we need to have an emotional audit. Under closer examination, we are able to see which of our ego states might need their core beliefs re-examined. The Parent, Adult and Child ego state model is the big kahuna, or rather, understanding our ego states is the big kahuna. In society, joy is often the emotion we expect or are expected to feel. The 'good' and 'right' emotion and definitely the one we 'should' be feeling on the first day of school. What was less acceptable is Riley feeling sadness and allowing herself to feel it. It was my sadness that had brought me to study counselling and, as I sat and listened to Bella, I started to get in touch with other sad memories. We all did. We need all our emotions and there are no good or bad ones. Learning to understand these different parts of ourselves, and how to relate to them is the integration we need. What we seek to find in the therapy room is often what our families did not know themselves to teach us and so we begin the higher education of the self.

Exercises

1. Think about what the Child part of you might be made up of? What emotions do you feel when it speaks to you? How do you remember experiencing your parents when you were growing up?
2. When has the Adapted Child had to hide their true feelings? When has the Free Child felt free enough to do what they wanted?
3. Now think about the relationships in your life you would like to change. How do your ego states influence your relationships?

Reference

Berne, E. (1961). *Transactional Analysis in Psychotherapy: A Systematic Individual and Social Psychiatry*. New York: Grove Press.

3

Strokes and *An Officer and a Gentleman*

Theory: Strokes

A psychological theory from transactional analysis where a 'stroke' is defined as a 'fundamental unit of recognition' (Berne 1964, p. 15). An essential ingredient in how humans interact. A stroke is also described as 'any act implying recognition of another's presence' (Berne 1964, p. 15).

Movie: *An Officer and a Gentleman (1982)*

After his Mum commits suicide, Zack Mayo is sent as a young boy to live with his wayward father, Byron, a petty officer in the Navy stationed in the Philippines. Years later, now a young man, Zack enrols in military aviation school to become a jet pilot, to his father's disbelief. Zack bonds quickly with another officer candidate, Sid Worley, and the boys start dating local girls, Paula and Lynette. Marine Gunnery Sergeant Foley, the boys' drill instructor, is tough and demanding, warning the boys about the domestic aspirations of the local girls. It is well known that many of the local girls dream that one day the intimate relationships they have with the officers will lead to marrying a pilot and escaping their small-town life. Zack wrestles to last the 13 weeks of training whilst coping with falling in love, the suicide of his best friend and facing his own inner demons.

What We're Doing

In this chapter, we will be looking at the psychological theory of strokes by closely examining the interactions between the characters in the movie *An Officer and a Gentleman*. By understanding the characters' relationship to Eric Berne's theory of strokes, we learn more about why they behave the way they do. Using my own experience in training, I invite you to consider how the theory may relate to your life.

We first observe the importance of strokes as a baby. We now know that the growth hormone levels of babies and their muscular activity are processes regulated by touch. The simple act of comfort through touch is essential to human survival. Non-verbal regulation is our first stroke; holding, touching, and caressing are the types of touch we offer when trying to soothe a baby but are also crucial in developing our orbitofrontal cortex, the area of the brain responsible for emotional regulation (Gerhardt 2004). As we grow and mature, our methods of stroking also mature. We move from non-verbal to verbal, and are now able to connect with people in a whole new way. As we grow the different areas of our brain, our capacity for connection with others and the world we inhabit also grows. Learning to understand how we engage in more complex forms of stroking enables us to better understand how we emotionally regulate, what we as unique individuals need and also how we can become dysregulated.

Negative Verbal Strokes

As a young boy, meeting his biological father Byron for the first time, Zack blames him for his mother's suicide. '*She believed you, she waited for you,*' are expressions of a young boy's confused response to one of the most painful human experiences – the loss of a significant attachment relationship. His father denies that his relationship with Zack's mother was anything serious, denouncing her expectations as a '*female lie.*' This is a negative verbal stroke given with the intention of being harsh and of rejecting Zack's attachment needs.

When Zack tells Byron he joined the Navy, Byron laughs. '*That's like saying you're gonna run for president. Officers don't have tattoos.*' This is another negative verbal stroke, which is hurtful to Zack who wants his father to respond from a Nurturing Parent ego state (Chapters 1, 2 and 9) and show his support and belief in his son.

Negative Non-verbal Strokes

Zack has not been in the Philippines for long when a group of boys take him to a secluded area and beat him up. They are fuelled by anger towards a white officer's child. The local boys assume Zack's privilege and their resentment stems from how the Filipinos are treated by the White officers and the shame which comes from being viewed as less important than another human being.

Positive Verbal Strokes

When Zack meets an attractive young woman, Paula, at the officer's candidate dance, he is startled by how a stranger can offer such encouraging words. Talking about whether he will last the training, Paula says, '*It'll happen. You just gotta see yourself making it.*' Zack is not used to hearing or receiving positive verbal strokes.

Paula's mother, a local girl herself who has had her own experience with falling in love with an officer's candidate – Paula's father – warns Paula not to chase Zack when she is in an emotionally vulnerable state. She warns that, as Paula's friend Lynette has done with Sid, Paula will end up doing and saying anything to trap Zack and make him stay and marry her. The trap she speaks of is to lie and say she is pregnant. Lynette lies to Sid thinking that the pregnancy will entice Sid to stay and to provide the strokes that a baby needs to survive. Lynette hopes her lie will be received as a positive verbal stroke invoking ideas of responsibility, love and family, which is exactly how Sid hears it.

Positive Non-verbal Strokes

Paula's eye contact and tone are positive non-verbal strokes, authentic and sincere qualities Zack is not used to. He responds by stroking her cheek as he smiles – another positive non-verbal stroke. Their relationship quickly becomes physical and the film highlights their connection and ability to comfort each other sexually with intimately shot scenes. Sex is a way adults receive and give strokes. These strokes can also sometimes become a replacement for the meaningful kinds of strokes a person might also want and need from a relationship.

Negative Conditional Verbal Strokes

When Zack first arrives in the Philippines to meet his father, a man he knows nothing about, he is already carrying a painful and shattered parental fantasy, the fantasy of the mother who stays alive to mother her child. Zack is grieving the shocking death of his mother and in a new country, he hears his father say, '*I don't have time for this Daddy stuff because that's not who I am.*' The unspoken condition here is 'accept me for the man I am and maybe we can stay in a relationship.' Flash forward, and as an adult, we see that Byron has introduced Zack to a life where they both engage in sexual experiences with multiple women. Referring to an evening they shared together, Byron says, *'Not as wild as when we banged those three stewardesses in Manila.'*

Zack has had to put away his needs of a father and mother, the fantasy of the yearned unconditional relationship, and has had to adjust to the real world where his father will spend time with him engaging in very specific activities centering around alcohol and sex. In the absence of positive strokes, he will accept the negative strokes his father offers him just to have his father in his life. In life, many of our relationships become conditional, and parent and child relationships are often the first experiences of this conditional love.

Positive Conditional Verbal Strokes

When Zack hears Byron say he's not cut out to be Zack's daddy, his response to his father's rejection of his paternal responsibility is, *'That's ok.'* Zack does not have many options. This man is all he has left of family in the world, and he will do whatever he needs to do to receive strokes, again preferring to receive a negative stroke rather than no stroke at all.

When Sid quits the training programme, he proposes to Lynette and hopes to return with her to his hometown of Oklahoma and raise their family. Lynette is shocked that Sid has quit the training three weeks before graduation. *'But I thought you understood – I want to marry a pilot,'* she says. Lynette offers Sid the positive stroke of saying 'Yes' to his marriage proposal, but it is conditional on Sid becoming an officer, giving Lynette the opportunity she is looking for – to leave her small town and be the wife of a pilot overseas.

Negative Unconditional Verbal Strokes

When Foley discovers Zack has been running a side hustle of buying pre-polished boots and belt buckles from the locals and turning a profit by selling them onto officers come the time of their regular uniform inspections, he is enraged and removes all Zack's weekend privileges. He spends the time personally forcing Zack to undergo gruelling physical exercise, pushing him to quit the training. At one point, Zack is doing push-ups in the rain and is asked to lower his face into the mud with Foley whispering, *'Deep down inside you know all these other boys and girls are better than you.'*

Positive Unconditional Verbal Strokes

At graduation, officers recite the oath where they pledge allegiance to the Constitution, 'to *support and defend against all enemies foreign and domestic.*' The line, '*I take this obligation freely*' might suggest that this verbal stroke they recite is unconditional. How free is an officer's candidate really, who must serve at the will and decision of a country and if for whatever reason they disagree, are dishonorably discharged? And yet, even in an oath recited by thousands of people over decades, there is a fine line between conditional and unconditional.

Paula tells her mother how she feels about Zack, '*I love him.*' Paula decides she will not trap Zack to be with her because she loves him unconditionally which means letting him go if that is what he wants.

Zack says to Paula, '*I wanted to thank you.*' He wants to say more but holds back, knowing his words are partly driven by jealousy after seeing Paula with another man. Simply thanking her with nothing else attached allows the stroke to be offered and received as an unconditional stroke.

Lynette sees that after completing the training, Zack has in fact returned to Paula of his own volition and Paula did not have to trap him to manipulate his affections. Lynette is sad for herself but truly happy for her friend. We see her cheering for Paula and crying with happiness, shouting, '*Way to go, Paula!*'

Positive Unconditional Non-verbal Strokes

When Zack struggles in aerodynamics class, he looks around the room and sees his classmates engrossed in their calculations. Flailing, he catches Sid's eye and, without even needing to ask, Sid lifts up the page of his book so Zack can see the answers. Later on, we hear Zack describe Sid as the '*best friend to everybody.*' We can infer that Sid would have helped out anyone in need, unconditionally.

During physical training, Seegar, the only girl in the group, struggles to climb a tall wall with the aid of a rope. She has, in fact, never been able to complete this part of the circuit. Meanwhile, Zack is the best in the class. On the day Zack is attempting to achieve the fastest timing on record, he sees Seegar struggling. Seegar's struggle is predictable, but what is new is Zack abandoning his one chance at the record for his own gain and instead doubling back to help Seegar get over the wall.

Counterfeit

Counterfeit strokes are the name we give to strokes that might sound good but feel bad. For example, when Foley puts Zack through the weekend of physical punishment, he tries to weaken his resolve as Zack is doing his push-ups.

'*Why don't we quit this little charade over a couple of beers at TJ's?*' A couple of beers together might sound like a nice idea, but the word charade, Foley's demeaning tone of voice, sneering facial expressions and intimidating body language are what makes the stroke counterfeit.

When Sid's father, also an officer, takes Sid and Zack out for dinner, he says, '*You boys are lucky you weren't in the programme when I was in it. You couldn't just quit the way you can now.*' It begins with the boys being told they are lucky, fortunate even, but ends with Sid's father deciding that the training they are getting is easy, less rigorous and not as legitimate as his experience, so it becomes a negative stroke.

Strokes in Families

The family we are born into teaches us everything we first know, and don't know, about strokes. These lessons in strokes are learnt verbally and non-verbally; a mix of positive and negative, conditional and unconditional. A human being's need for social connection is biological and we sometimes accept negative strokes in the absence of positive strokes simply to feel any stroke at all, some semblance of connection with another. As children, we focus on survival; what we need physiologically and emotionally to survive our environment. We also learn how to get what we need by what is modelled for us, what we absorb and notice from those around us.

As Zack learns to open himself up, to trust himself and the world a little more, he learns to give and receive different strokes, ones that will allow him to lead a more meaningful life. Sad and upset that Sid is leaving school, he tries to make a case for his friend to Foley. '*He's the best candidate in the class, the best student, the best leader, the best friend to everybody.*' Giving a positive stroke is not easy for Zack, as this means he must get in touch with feelings of love for his friend, feelings that leave him vulnerable, and love has been nothing but painful for Zack.

When Lynette breaks up with Sid after he drops out of school, Sid hangs himself in the bathroom of a motel. For Zack, in the absence of positive, unconditional verbal and non-verbal strokes, he has learnt to blame himself as a way to cope and now falls back on this strategy to manage the pain and loss of his second significant attachment relationship. Paula tells Zack, '*You didn't kill your mother, you didn't kill Sid, they killed themselves.*' Paula is offering Zack a positive, unconditional verbal stroke, but it will take Zack some time to be able to hear it. He will need to process his own anger and sadness first.

'*I don't want you to love me. I don't want anyone to love me. I don't need you, I don't need a Navy, I don't need anybody.*'

How we learn to give and receive strokes impacts the decisions we make and the quality of our interpersonal relationships. Zack finds it hard to receive positive, unconditional strokes. For Zack, intimacy is an unconscious reminder of the loss of a significant attachment figure. To protect himself, he filters the strokes he allows himself to feel, and also filters the strokes he gives out, preferring to '*cut it off.*' He cuts himself off from the feeling but also from people. When he graduates, he throws his hat in the air and looks around. He is alone. Remaining distant and avoidant, he realises how detrimental this behaviour has been on his relationships and the quality of his life.

Like a family, different cultures have their own non-verbal rules about giving and receiving certain strokes over others. Sometimes the cultural message could be 'don't talk about emotions.' The Navy has this cultural message, so when Zack says to Foley at his graduation, '*I won't ever forget you, Sergeant. I wouldn't have made it if it weren't for you,*' he is taking control of the strokes he gives out rather than following a cultural legacy.

As the weeks of my training went by, I noticed how different topics affected each of us in a different way. There were weekends when some of us would leave the training positively pumped and on a real high. Then there were weekends when some of us had become quiet – gone inward or to another place – long before the day had come to an end. That was me on the weekend we learnt about strokes. When Bella told us to think about the strokes we might have received in our family, I thought about the non-verbal rules around asking for certain strokes. Asking for a stroke you wanted was seen as shaming the person or being ungrateful for what was given. Culturally, there was an attitude of 'giving someone a big head' if you told them how wonderful they were. Asking for strokes was considered exposing, making yourself vulnerable to another person by telling them they had the power to give you a stroke that would mean something to you. Strangely, there were times I remembered my parents even rejecting a stroke I knew they wanted, like a hug! Growing up as an Asian girl in Britain, there were often times that strokes were given which I did not want but I was not allowed to reject them. For instance, being praised for laying the table and having to conceal my feeling of fury because I did not understand why I was asked but never my male cousins. I did not want that stroke but culturally I was expected to accept it and be happy about it. And giving yourself strokes, the most demonstrative illustration of which was masturbation was definitely not encouraged.

Claude Steiner examined the myth in families around giving and receiving strokes and referred to the control exhibited as 'basic training for lovelessness' (Steiner 1971, p. 114).

Don't Give Strokes
Don't Ask for Strokes
Don't Accept Strokes
Don't Reject Strokes
Don't Give Yourself Strokes

(Steiner 1971, p. 115)

Exercises

1. Examine the nature of the strokes given in your family by your parents, siblings and other family members of significance.
2. Which strokes do you freely give and receive in your life?
3. Identify the strokes you do not talk about and why?

References

Berne, E. (1964). *Games People Play*. England: Penguin.

Gerhardt, S. (2004). *Why Love Matters*. East Sussex: Brunner-Routledge.

Steiner, C. (1971). *Scripts People Live*. NY: Grove Press.

Transactions and *My Fair Lady*

Theory: Transactions

Eric Berne (1961) describes the way we relate to each other as being a series of transactions. Berne describes a transaction as 'an exchange of strokes,' and the 'unit of social intercourse.' Looking at and analysing the transactions in human interaction formed the basis of transactional analysis.

Movie: *My Fair Lady (1964)*

In 1938, *My Fair Lady* was adapted from the 1913 play by George Bernard Shaw, *Pygmalion*, and put to music by American composer Frederick Loewe. Set in the early 1900s, the story centres around the life of one Eliza Dolittle, a charming and high-spirited cockney flower girl working in the East End of London. An encounter between Eliza and phonetician Professor Henry Higgins leads to a bet between Higgins and his friend, Colonel Pickering, as to whether Higgins really has the ability to turn Eliza into a genteel English-speaking 'lady' able to pass as such in high society. Eliza moves into Higgins' house and the challenge begins.

What We're Doing

In this chapter, we will be looking at the psychological theory of transactions viewed through the movie, *My Fair Lady*. As we learn about the nature and purpose of transactions through our characters, we start to understand something about our own interactions in the world. Using my own experience in training, I invite you to consider how the theory may relate to your life.

Though I found myself studying Transactional Analysis, it didn't begin that way and, as with all good stories, it began with a setback. Unsure about which course to select, I chose Integrative Psychotherapy, where what was offered was the opportunity to learn about many different psychotherapy modalities. This seemed, as Higgins might say, a bloody good place to start. All decided, fired up and prepared to go, I had been told the Integrative Course was full up and did I want to register for next year's intake? No, I did not. I was ready now. And so, with every intention of beginning some kind of training in some kind of modality, I shuffled my enthusiasm along to the Transactional Analysis course where there is one spot left. Did I know anything about Transactional Analysis, I was asked by the course convenor. No, I did not.

Eric Berne was an experienced psychiatrist, en route to becoming a psychoanalyst, but as attested to in Jorgenson and Jorgenson's biography (1984), to Berne's grave disappointment, and despite his substantial clinical knowledge and training, his application to become a psychoanalyst was refused. At this point, Berne had already begun his psychoanalytically informed work on ego states and the Parent, Adult and Child model and it was from here that Transactional Analysis as a modality was born. Every birth has an element of violence contained within it. The journey of the foetus travelling down the birth canal and being expelled from the comfort of the mother's body into the outside world is, at its most primal level, a violent shock for both mother and child and requires enormous resilience from both. Being violently rejected from the Psychoanalytic Institute at this stage in his career was emotional for Berne and it was from his fall and his subsequent resilience that he birthed Transactional Analysis.

'*She is a human being,*' Pickering says to Higgins, reminding Higgins that despite investing in 'Project Eliza,' he must realise that she is a person and needs to be treated with respect. Ironically, Higgins has earlier reminded Eliza of the very same but he had done so with a caveat. Her humanness relied on her proper pronunciation of the English language. '*Remember that you are a human being with a soul and the divine gift of articulate speech.*' On hearing her speak in her particular vernacular, Higgins says, '*A woman who utters such disgusting and depressing noises has no right to be anywhere, no right to live.*'

Transactions are made up of a stimulus and a response. The stimulus begins the transaction and the response allows it to continue. Like this, we can continue transacting or conversing with each other. There are three main categories of transactions: complementary, crossed and ulterior.

As you read through the chapter, notice if you are reminded of relationship interactions from your own life.

Complementary Transactions

HIGGINS: *Do you know Colonel Pickering – the author of Spoken Sanskrit?*
PICKERING: *I am Colonel Pickering – who are you?*
HIGGINS: *I'm Henry Higgins – author of Higgins' Universal Alphabet.*
PICKERING: *I came from India to meet you!*
HIGGINS: *I was going to India to meet you!*

Understanding ego states (Chapters 1, 2 and 9) is useful to interpret what type of transaction is taking place. For example, the first three lines of the Higgins/Pickering exchange above can be seen to be transactions from the Adult ego state (Fig. 4.1). The two that follow are a combination of the Adult and the Free Child. In all five lines of dialogue, Pickering and Higgins are transacting from the same ego state as each other.

We can also have a complementary transaction where two different ego states are transacting.

HIGGINS: *Where are you staying?*
PICKERING: *At the Carlton.*
HIGGINS: *No you're not, you're staying at 27a Wimpole Street. You come along with me. We'll have a little jaw over supper.*
PICKERING: *Right you are.*

Here, Higgins begins in his Adult ego state but then switches into Critical Parent, albeit a seemingly generous one, where he overrides Pickering's choices and tells him what he intends for him to do instead. This is as opposed to enquiring if living with Higgins is something Pickering would want to do. In removing his autonomy and assuming responsibility, a behaviour we expect from a parent to a child, Higgins moves out of Adult (Fig. 4.2). The scene ends with Pickering walking happily to Higgins' house.

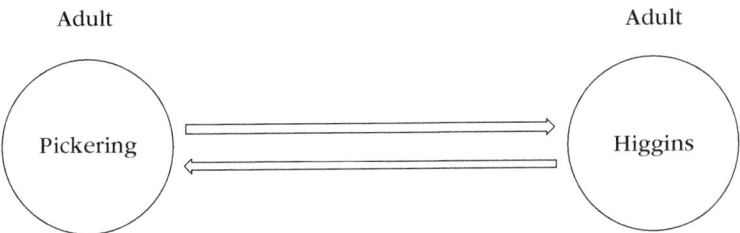

Fig. 4.1 Complementary Transactions Between Adult and Adult

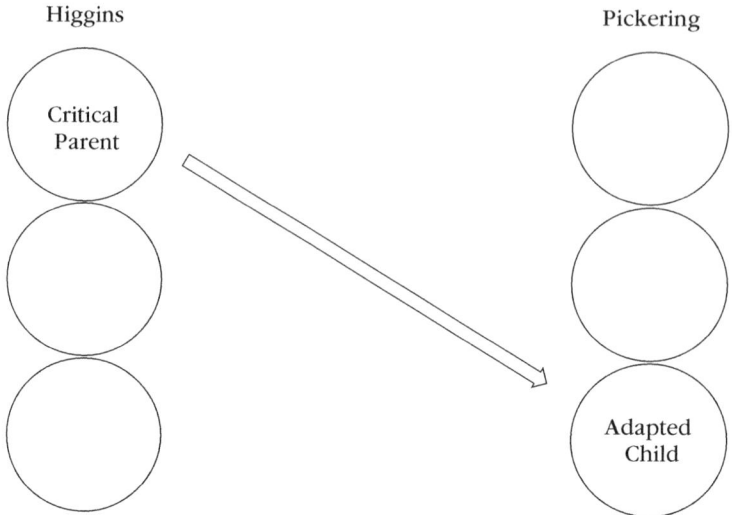

Fig. 4.2 Complementary Transactions from Critical Parent to Adapted Child

Sometimes our Adult is happy with the outcome and so we continue to have Parent/Child transactions, doing so in awareness. The reason the transaction remains complementary is that we are to assume Pickering is content on some level to transact from his Adapted Child and be told what to do. There is a quality of familiarity with complementary transactions, and in this way, Pickering and Higgins can continue to transact in this manner. Higgins is exerting control with Pickering agreeing to acquiesce, indefinitely. Certain expectations and assumptions exist within this type of transaction that ensure its smoothness and continuation.

What we do not know is whether Pickering's Child ego state felt unable in that moment to voice that he would much rather stay at The Carlton despite his new friend's exuberance and their shared professional camaraderie, and whether Pickering might have wished to find another way they could meet for a chat over dinner. If this is the case, and Pickering agreeing to Higgins' idea suggests a loss of voice then something else is going on. Is Pickering transacting with Higgins whilst his Child is being reminded of his domineering father with whom he could not disagree? Many codependent relationships (Chapter 11) transact using complementary transactions.

Does Higgins transact from his Critical Parent because his domineering mother allowed him no space to think for himself? Note that the internalised Critical Parent may exert control in ways which appear nurturing, for example, the offering of a meal and lodgings. The transaction remains complementary as long as the ego states from and to which the transactions are sent, remain the same. The term complementary should not be interpreted to mean that the transactions only occur in healthy awareness. They could be in healthy awareness, and also might not be, and still remain complementary.

Crossed Transactions

After their first meeting on the street, Higgins has tossed some loose change on the ground for Eliza. This is money Higgins is happy to part with and which will not remotely impact his financial status. This is not the case for Eliza who has for a moment become rich as a result of Higgins' offhand gesture. Eliza thinks about the bet that Higgins voiced to Pickering, made with conviction but with no present sign of execution, regarding turning Eliza into a lady and someone who has a significantly more financially comfortable life. She decides that she will make it happen and turns up at Higgins' house. She wants him to do what is necessary so she can earn more money for herself.

The butler answers the door and says, '*Name, please.*' Eliza answers, '*My name is of no concern to you whatsoever.*' The butler asks for Eliza's name as that is part of his job and he is transacting from his Adult ego state. Eliza, however, does not respond from her Adult but from her Critical Parent. She fears revealing her identity too quickly will result in a quick ousting into the street, so she withholds her name until she is further inside the house and thereby closer to Higgins to make her case. The idea of 'Project Eliza' begins to excite Higgins, but as the details of Eliza's elocution are discussed, Eliza gets scared that she is being asked for a large sum of money she does not have. Her emotional response is fear, which elicits an emotional response of anger from Higgins.

HIGGINS: *Somebody's going to touch you with a broomstick if you don't stop snivelling. Sit down!'*
ELIZA: *Anybody would think you were my father.*

Higgins transacts from his Critical Parent ego state, but despite sitting down when she is told, Eliza's words do not come from her Adapted Child, responding instead from her Adult ego state. In doing this, Eliza offers Higgins a crossed transaction. The complementary ego state to respond from here would be the Adapted Child as this is the ego state to which Higgins' transaction has been sent. What Eliza does next, her response to Higgins, is not complementary it is crossed. The emotional temperature here is that Higgins and Eliza are indeed cross/angry but it is not the emotion we are referring to when we look at what constitutes the crossed transaction. It is the crossing of the ego states which is the important part. The fact that Eliza happens to draw attention to the Parent ego state with her words by comparing Higgins to her father is by coincidence. Crossing Higgins' transaction by transacting

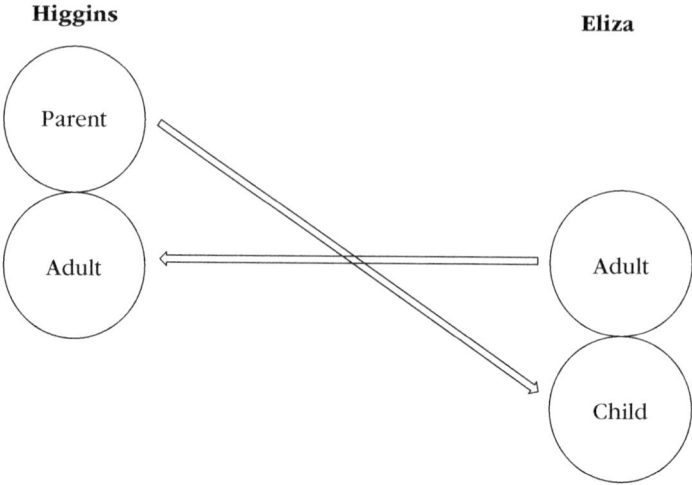

Fig. 4.3 Crossed Transactions

from her Adult, she sends a message to Higgins' Adult that she refuses to be complicit in his treatment of her as a child. He then calms down. The arrows in Fig. 4.3 show how the transactions cross.

There are many reasons why we might want to opt out of complementary transactions and choose a crossed transaction instead. In Eliza's decision to do this, she is saying to Higgins, 'I will not be shamed by you.' The Critical Parent can use the act of shaming to communicate their message or information. By moving into her Adult ego state, Eliza's Child does not absorb the shame and does not adapt.

Whilst we are learning about transacting in healthy awareness, we also can sometimes feel shame when we decide to offer a crossed transaction. When we behave in a way someone else is not expecting or that they are unhappy with, we can often experience shame in not behaving in the 'correct' way and perhaps feel or even be told that we are doing the 'wrong' thing. This kind of shame is transitory and passes the more we practice transacting consciously and in awareness, understanding the parts of us that are in need of healing and of developing an awareness of our own emotional internal world. It is through learning to transact consciously that we start to heal and shift patterns of dysfunctional behaviour that, as Professor Higgins might say, we have grown accustomed to.

Ulterior Transactions

Professor Higgins is a focussed individual. Committed and passionate about speech and the English language. He could also be described as rigid, obsessive, misogynistic and even cruel. Noting Eliza is scared and about to leave, he deliberately promises her chocolate in hopes she will be tempted to stay.

HIGGINS: *You'll have boxes of them, barrels every day. You'll live on them, eh?*
ELIZA: *I wouldn't of ate it only I'm too ladylike to take it out of my mouth.*

Looking at this transaction out of context, it seems without cruelty. Maybe even kind. Moments prior to these words, Higgins has just announced that after he finishes the bet, he plans to toss Eliza back into the same gutter he found her in. On hearing this, Eliza accuses him of not having a heart and is about to leave when Higgins offers her chocolates, a commodity not easily available to a flower girl and an obvious bribe to stay. His body posture is manipulative and threatening, and when the words are put together in context with other elements such as motivation, tone and history, we see him as overtly duplicitous and we have ourselves an ulterior transaction. On the social level, it appears that Higgins is transacting from his Nurturing Parent and that this message is responded to by Eliza's Adapted Child. If we examine the matter more closely, we can see that Higgins is covertly transacting from his Critical Parent. He is uninterested in listening to Eliza or indeed understanding that she feels disrespected, but will do and say what he thinks will get him what he wants.

Eliza does stay, and her relationship with Higgins evolves. They both learn about themselves by being in a relationship with the other. Higgins learns that his attitude towards women must be updated, allowing for the fact that he did not expect to find himself developing loving feelings for Eliza. He is forced to entertain a point of view other than his own, an important aspect in transacting with people to achieve healthy functioning relationships. Higgins believed that Eliza would free herself from the shackles of class by speaking English in a certain manner, but in finding her way into high society, Eliza developed a self-realisation that transcended class prejudices. In becoming a lady of society, Eliza learned lessons not only in language but in self-worth. On the night Higgins wins the bet, there is technically no more reason for Eliza to remain living in his house. Eliza has tuned into the way she feels about Higgins – that she loves this infuriating man – long before Higgins has himself become aware of how he feels about her.

Social Level:

HIGGINS (CRITICAL PARENT): *You shouldn't have said that, Eliza, that shows a want of feeling.*
ELIZA (ADAPTED CHILD): *I'm sorry. I'm only a common ignorant girl. In my station I have to be careful. There can't be any feelings between the likes of you and the likes of me.*

On the social level, Higgins appears to be transacting from Critical Parent and Eliza responding from Adapted Child. Higgins is having a conversation he doesn't want to have and is about to lose his temper, something he rarely does. He is feeling dysregulated and rattled that Eliza is showing visible signs of being cross with him. He does not understand yet that he has deeper feelings for her. Eliza is devastated by his behaviour all evening and feels as if she does not matter to Higgins at all.

On a covert level, the ulterior transaction is Higgins transacting from his Adapted Child (sad and confused), and Eliza responding from her Critical Parent (passive-aggressive and sarcastic). When we are dealing with ulterior transactions, it is the covert rather than the social messages that will influence the result of the transaction. Below are the emotional motivations driving the above conversation.

Ulterior Level:

HIGGINS (ADAPTED CHILD): *You hurt me.*
ELIZA (CRITICAL PARENT):   *You hurt me.*

In reality, we move between crossed, complementary and ulterior transactions in both functional and dysfunctional relationships every day. If we can understand how it is we transact with people, we can understand how we might be able to better communicate. The more we understand what we are feeling, the more we can see what we are doing. This helps us learn how we might voluntarily and involuntarily disengage from communication via crossed and/or ulterior transactions. It helps us understand how we might miss getting what we need or get stuck doing what we do not want to do via complementary transactions.

In my new school, making friends felt challenging. It made me wonder about how to do it. And whether that aspect of attaching should have felt more instinctive. I watched the groups from a distance. I heard and saw laughter that emanated easily like steam off a cup of coffee, bodies in motion that somehow knew where to drift, towards who and how and when. Inside my own body, I wanted to be in a group of friends that chatted after class with ease and purpose. I wanted to reflexively know where to walk and to who and when and how to engage in these transactions. So when a new girl, whose name I did not know but who I recognised from my class, asked if I wanted to come with her and others for lunch, it was interesting to hear the words that came out of my mouth (illustrated in Fig. 4.4).

Social Level:

NEW GIRL (ADULT): *Want to go for lunch with me and the girls?*
ME (ADULT):   *I have some stuff to do at lunch, but I'll see you later.*

Ulterior Level:

NEW GIRL (NURTURING PARENT): *You seem lonely.*
ME (ADAPTED CHILD):   *I'm scared.*

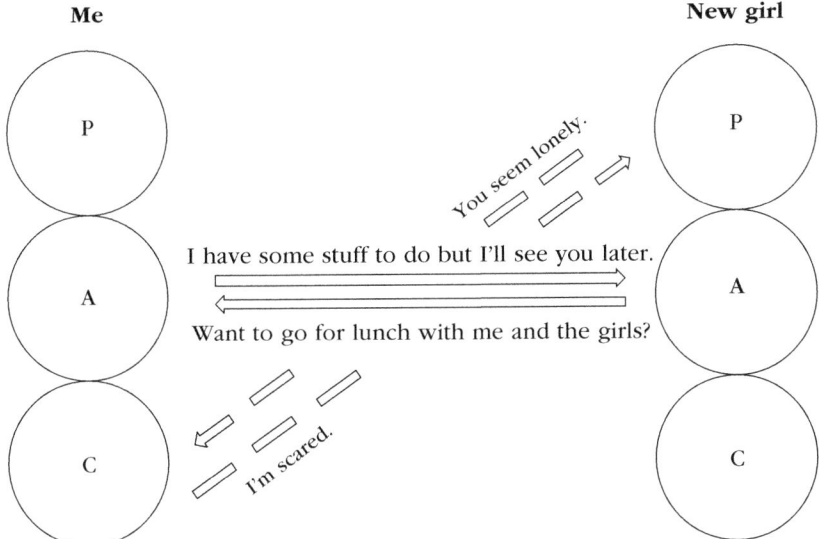

Fig. 4.4 Ulterior Transactions

Despite communication being 70% non-verbal, Higgins was on to something with his obsession over language. As with Eliza, language can start by being a barrier to connection. But here in the material world, it is through language that we can be understood. With understanding, we have a connection. In connection, we can be seen. To be seen is to be witnessed. To be witnessed is existential recognition. The language of being alive.

Exercises

1. Consider a relationship in which you struggle. Are the transactions mostly complementary, crossed or ulterior?
2. Which transactions do you feel most comfortable using when communicating with this person?
3. Consider an ulterior transaction you might have engaged in. Identify the social and the covert message.

References

Berne, E. (1961). *Transactional Analysis in Psychotherapy: A Systematic Individual and Social Psychiatry*. New York: Grove Press.

Jorgenson, H.I. and Jorgenson, E.W. (1984). *Eric Berne, Master Gamesman; A Transactional Biography*. New York: Grove Press.

5

Hungers and *Parasite*

Theory: Hungers

The everyday problem of the human being is the structure of his waking hours – Eric Berne (1961, p. 85).

This is the psychological theory that there is a motivational force behind why people do what they do.

Movie: *Parasite (2019)*

In an impoverished part of Seoul lives the Kim family: Ki-taek and his wife, Choong-sook, their son Ki-woo and daughter Ki-jung. Their home is a cramped and mildewed lower-ground space, crawling with cockroaches. One day, Ki-woo inherits a high-paying tutor gig from his friend Min and starts working for the rich Park family. Quickly, the Kim family dishonestly insert themselves into the Park family's workforce, and with each insertion, the duplicity becomes more elaborate. One night, an unforeseen development becomes a problem for the Kims, and the consequences of their deception begin to unravel dramatically, resulting in the ultimate climactic event – death.

What We're Doing

In this chapter, we will be looking at the psychological theory of Hungers in the movie *Parasite*. As we learn about the model, we will use it to understand more about the motivations of the Kim family and the power of Hungers as a force in our lives. Using my own experience in training, I invite you to consider how the theory may relate to your life.

When we think of hunger, we immediately think of the physiological sensations we feel when the body is hungry – stomach pangs, a growling of the stomach, a feeling of emptiness. What happens just before we get these pangs and growls is the biological production and release of a hormone called ghrelin, the 'hunger hormone.' This hormone is what brings the body's hunger and our need for food into our awareness, setting us on the road to doing something about it (Pradhan et al. 2013). If we think about the moment we arrive into this world as newborns, we come with the critical need to feed. It is imperative that we find ways in which we can nourish ourselves with food so we can grow. Our hunger serves as the sign we need to attend to what is a priority for our survival. Caregivers don't just give newborn babies food to help them develop. We also hold them to make contact, we play music to stimulate them, and we coo and smile so they recognise us. We now understand that these universal responses to the care of a newborn play a pivotal role in shaping the brain of the newborn. Contact, stimulation and recognition are all experiences which help develop the pre-frontal cortex, the area of the brain instrumental for our social interactions (Kolk and Rakic 2021).

Parasite opens with a tilted-angle view of the street through the lower-ground window of the family's apartment. The teenagers are told by their father to hold their phones high and explore all possible crevices to try and piggyback onto someone else's Wi-Fi connection. Ki-woo and Ki-jung climb onto an internal parapet wall in the toilet, arms outstretched above them. Choong-sook kicks Ki-taek, a brutish yet loving jab, to wake him just as the street fumigation truck arrives. Ki-taek says not to close the window so the family are able to benefit from free pest control for their insect infestation. As the family chokes from the toxic fumes, Ki-taek remains unperturbed, his eyes fixated on the YouTube demonstration video where a girl shows how to construct pizza boxes in record time. We are less than five minutes into the film and the extremity of sensations experienced by the Kim family is palpable. I am wondering about Recognition Hunger for this family, for their self-esteem, and I suspect this is the director's intention. Their home has them hunched under low ceilings, almost physically folded in half to fit within it and I wonder about the impact of this way of living and if it has served to minimise their existence. How does society recognise them? With the aid of his sister Ki-jung's expert forgery skills, Ki-woo lies to his new employers, the Park family, about being a college student and fake certificates from Oxford University convince the Park family they can trust him. The wife views the forged certificates just long enough to say she is uninterested in them and simply requires him to be as good as his predecessor, Min, with who they were very happy. The name 'Oxford University' has already provided the required level of recognition that the Park family hungers for, enabling her to pretend the name does not matter.

Our tutor Bella writes on the board: Contact Hunger, Stimulus Hunger, Recognition Hunger, Incident Hunger, Sexual Hunger and Structure Hunger. She divides the room into six areas representing the six Hungers and asks us all to go to the section we feel is the Hunger we relate to the most. We do not move immediately. It makes me curious as to whether there is shame in being Hungry. If there is something that feels hard to admit in acknowledging, 'this is where I did not get enough.' Or even, 'where I feel I might not be enough.' The whole group splits between Contact, Stimulus and Recognition. Nobody stands in Incident, Sexual or Structure. What is this about? Is Eric Berne, the founder of Transactional Analysis, outdated? Or is there more to the story?

In *Parasite*, once Ki-woo is established as a tutor for the Park's family teenage daughter, Da-hye, he proceeds to offer his 'cousin's friend' – in truth, actually his sister – to Mrs. Park as an art teacher for her boisterous son, Da-song. Once Ki-woo and Ki-jung are both working for the Park family, they begin finding ways to bring their parents into the scheme. Ki-jung plants her panties in the car and when Mr. Park finds them, he assumes his driver has been using his car for sex – a sackable offence. Ki-jung casually offers her 'uncle's friend' – her father – as a new driver. To bring their mother in, they must also eject the housekeeper who has been a fixture in the house for years. She was inherited by the Park family as she worked for the previous owner and architect of the house. Discovering she is highly allergic to peaches, Ki-jung scrapes the peach fuzz off the fruit and delicately sprinkles the powder onto her neck. Ki-taek tells Mrs. Park he saw the housekeeper in the local hospital being diagnosed with tuberculosis. A moment later, and after years of service, the housekeeper is on the street with her bags packed and Choong-sook has replaced her, gleefully walking the corridors with plates of freshly cut peaches.

The decisions being made by the Kim family are cruel but also creative. The cruelty of their actions outweighs the creativity but it is their desperation, their Hunger that drives them.

Contact Hunger

When Ki-woo's friend Min first suggests he take over tutoring Da-hye while Min goes abroad, Ki-woo's first response is, '*Why ask a loser like me?*' Min explains that he has a romantic interest in Da-hye and does not trust the other boys like he trusts Ki-woo. However, Da-hye and Ki-woo quickly become romantically involved, '*She really likes me too,*' he tells his family. To be liked and noticed is partly Ki-woo's Recognition Hunger but he also wants the contact with Da-hye, he sees a future with her.

The Kim family functions emotionally closely together in their own home but also in an unauthorised evening of criminal debauchery in the Park's home. They enjoy the contact of being together. They enjoy each other's company in a way that the physically and emotionally disconnected Park family cannot and do not. For all their money and privilege, Mr. and Mrs. Park have had to force their daughter to come on their camping trip whilst the marital relationship between Mr. and Mrs. Park sees Mrs. Park as timid and Mr. Park as ambivalent.

Stimulus Hunger

As humans, we have a biological need to engage our senses in the wider world in which we live; to taste, to hear, to smell, to touch and to see. The extreme contrasts between the two families are a consistent motif throughout the film and yet the families are similar in their need for stimulation as they all remain unnourished in different ways.

In the Kim's cramped basement there are scraps of food, the sound of drunks vomiting, the smell of toxic fumigation gas, the killing of stink bugs and the sight of people urinating. When the Park family go away on a camping trip, the Kim family make themselves at home. A long shot of the Kim family enjoying the forbidden pleasures of the Park family's life; the spacious interior and the expansive, manicured garden surrounded by a plethora of modern technological amenities. '*This is pretty classy, rain falling on the lawn as we sip our whisky.*' Close-ups of an abundance of rich food they cannot afford for themselves, '*wow, all these varieties of alcohol.*'

Recognition Hunger

It is Da-song, the Park's little boy, who mentions that Ki-taek, Choong-sook and Ki-jung all '*smell the same.*' Choong-sook baulks at the idea of doing four separate loads of laundry with four different kinds of washing soap to throw the Park family off the Kim family scent. The smell is of poverty and low hygiene as much as the stench of deceit. Ki-jung says that the issue is where they live – it is a '*semi-basement smell.*' Ki-taek, the eternal optimist, reminds them that they are fortunate to have such a problem to be concerned about. That in a society where '*an opening for a security guard attracts five hundred university graduates our entire family got hired.*'

Ki-woo daydreams about marrying Da-hye one day. Ki-taek immediately imagines his son inheriting the house they are now sitting in, without permission, daydreaming of his own recognition that will come via proximity to his future wealthy daughter-in-law.

KI-TAEK (TALKING ABOUT MRS. PARK):   *She's so naive and nice. She's rich but still nice.*

CHOONG-SOOK: *Not, 'rich, but still nice.' Nice because she's rich. You know? Hell, if I had all this money I'd be nice too.*

Structure Hunger

This is about how to organise ourselves in our daily life. How we achieve the things we want whilst we cope with all the elements of life we do not want. How does the Kim family achieve recognition whilst they struggle with classism and poverty? Berne identified six possible methods of psychological structural organisation.

1. **Withdrawal**: Choong-sook asks Ki-woo why he is lying down out-side. Ki-woo replies that he is '*gazing at the sky from home.*' He has withdrawn into himself, thinking about a life with Da-hye and the idea that the Park's home could be his own.
2. **Rituals**: Through familiar practice of human interaction, we learn an accepted manner of initial ritual. For example, we exchange pleasantries of introduction, where we might talk about the weather. It's brief and not particularly emotional, but safe. It also comes with assumptions and expectations that we hold to allow us to get to the next moment. Those rituals and assumptions go beyond simple introductory exchanges and seep into our behaviour and understanding of others. When Mr. Park found the panties in his car, he was confused. He assumed his driver had had sex in his car, but seemed more perturbed at the nature of a woman who could forget her panties. An earring he could understand, but panties must mean she was on drugs. Engaging in certain rituals calms us and makes us feel safe. Forgetting one's panties after an illicit sexual tryst felt worrying and unsafe for Mr. Park.
3. **Pastimes**: When the Kim family gets together, they talk, they dream, they hope, they visualise. They learn about what interests one another and these interactions create closeness. Pastiming lets us find out about our similarities and discover like-minded people where we can receive and offer positive strokes. Sometimes pastiming can lead to false beliefs and the idea that those you do not pastime with have nothing in common with you.

   Ki-taek: *Rich people are naive. No resentments.*
   Choong-sook: *No creases on them. It all gets ironed out. Money is an iron.*

4. **Activities**: The Park family camping trip and the Kim family's illicit dinner as a result of their camping trip.
5. **Games**: In the absence of positive strokes, humans tolerate and engage in negative strokes simply to stay in contact. This is referred to as games detailed in Berne's book, *Games People Play*. People are less satisfied with the end result, but are partially satisfied, as negative contact is perceived as better than no contact. When Choong-sook compares her husband to a cockroach, he does not feel good. He pretends to be on the verge of punching her, but the air, thick with

violent promise, soon breaks into hilarity. Ki-taek masks his anger with humour. The game, the pretence, is the charade; a foreshadowing of how the pain of feeling demeaned and belittled is much closer to the surface than might appear and more violent than anyone can tell. It hints at the tragedy to come.

6. **Intimacy**: When Ki-jung and Ki-woo are daydreaming of having a house like the Park's, Ki-taek seems troubled. To comfort himself, he says, *'We live here now, don't we? Getting drunk in the living room [. . .] This is our home right now. It's cosy.'* The delusion of the fantasy is a form of psychological intimacy that cuts off and protects Ki-taek from his stark and differing reality.

Incident Hunger

Feeling excited in life is about different experiences for all of us. Some incidents are unwanted and we seek to create a calmer environment for ourselves. For others, we crave incidents and this feeling gives us a sense of a forward-moving motion with our lives. Without any incident at all, we have stagnation, boredom, we cannot flourish and grow and move to the next phase in our life journey. It is about learning how to select and instigate the correct incidents for us.

Meeting the Park family felt like progress for the Kim family – up until the old housekeeper rang the doorbell. She says she has left behind something important that she must now collect. It transpires that the housekeeper had been hiding her husband in the basement for years. A frenetic and violent altercation ensues between the housekeeper and the Kim family as each threatens to expose the other.

Ki-taek asks the housekeeper's husband, *'how can you live in a place like this?'* *'What'll you do, you don't have a plan?'* The irony being that the Kim family have also been living in shocking conditions inside their own basement for years, but since meeting the Parks, Ki-taek feels they now have a plan. The housekeeper's husband has become so disoriented by spending years hidden away that he tells Ki-taek he feels comfortable. Without a suitable amount of Incident Hunger, his temporal cognition has been impaired, *'It feels like I was born here,'* he says.

Sexual Hunger

The second foreshadowing is seen where Mr. and Mrs. Park return sooner than expected from camping. Ki-taek, his son and daughter hide, scared and motionless under the coffee table. Unable to move for fear of being caught, they can do nothing but listen to Mr. Park discussing the smell he gets from Ki-taek. The verbal commentary is going on whilst he engages in sexual foreplay on the sofa with his wife. The potency of the offensive stench is compared to when you '*boil a rag*,' or the smell of people who are by class forced to ride the underground. Mr. Park observes Ki-taek coming close to '*crossing the line*' in his behaviour, but also notes that though he never does, the smell of him is too much. After Mr. Park fired his driver for apparent and inappropriate sexual practice in the back seat of the car, he comments to Mrs. Park that the two of them on the sofa that night is, '*like the back seat.*' Mr. Park asks Mrs. Park if she still has the panties he found in the car and suggests she wear them. Mrs. Park says, in whispered tones of sexual ecstasy, '*buy me drugs.*' This is in contrast to her loud, audible exclamation when she feared that the driver might have had a girl in her husband's car who could lose her panties and use drugs. The director deliberately, and with cinematic finesse, crosses lines of desire, disgust, shame, sex and social graces, illustrating our Sexual Hunger is as visceral as it is demonised.

What we hunger for, we are also sometimes ashamed of, and I am taken back to the exercise in school where not one person stood in the area designated Sexual Hunger.

After a tragic and violent night with the housekeeper, and an equally terrible deluge of rain, the Kim family return to their lower-ground apartment to find it submerged in sewage water. Flooding has forced hundreds of people in Seoul out of their dwellings into makeshift shelters. In a movie about a poverty-stricken semi-basement, an upper-class house of opulence and a secret bunker that connects three families' destinies, the river of sewage metaphorically heralds the overflowing collapse of all three.

The next morning, it is Da-song's birthday party. As Mrs. Park giggles on the telephone with her friends about an impromptu party of daytime drinking, the musical underscore becomes discordant and we can feel Ki-taek's response to her high-pitched laughing is without his usual patient fortitude towards his employer. As Mrs. Park sits in the back of the car with her feet up on the headrest, Ki-taek struggles to listen to her. She tells her friends on the telephone how thankful she is that the rain has cleared the sky of all pollution for their party. This same rain has meant the Kim family, along with hundreds of others, no longer have a home. Mrs. Park rolls down the window as Ki-taek becomes humiliatingly aware of how the night of sewage has intensified his own smell.

Our tutor Bella gives us each a set of different coloured numbers comprising two, three, four, five and six. She asks which Hungers we would choose if we could have more than one. Slowly we moved across the room using our numbers as representatives to occupy our space. I could see that what we needed before was permission to admit and acknowledge our multiple Hungers, the idea of having more than one had been shameful. Incident, Sexual and Structure were no longer empty but full of numbers/ people. A memory floats up from the debris which I had not thought about in years of being the only Asian family in an all-white area of Surrey where I grew up. I always noticed the wrinkled noses of the white men in the pub where my father would drink when they smelt the curry on his clothes and the confusing way I experienced how they treated him after a couple of drinks, both overly familiar and rudely dismissive. They made jokes I never laughed at but that created a burning sensation of rage inside my body. There were years of disorienting comments about our skin colour, the smell of our clothes, drunk people saying 'I could murder a curry,' girls moving away from me on the bus 'not wanting to sit next to a Paki.' I wondered about the impact of such pervasive shame on my Recognition Hunger.

When we do not acknowledge our individual Hungers and find healthy ways to satisfy them, we push our desires down. We use the emotion of disgust to help us cope with the feelings of shame that we do not have what we need. The suppression of Hungers can lead to psychological attempts to feel whole and cope with an unconscious sense of fragmentation which can in turn lead to physical symptoms like depression or anxiety.

In an attempt to subdue the housekeeper from exposing them, Ki-taek accidentally kills her. The housekeeper's husband is bereft with rage and kills Ki-jung. Ki-taek sees Mr. Park take a sniff in the air around the house-keeper's husband, which is enough to trigger all the feelings of shame and rage Ki-taek has suppressed within him for years, even from others, all buried underneath a mask and cheerful demeanour. All the Hungers he has neglected cannot be sated as he drives a knife into Mr. Park.

Parasite is a social satire but also a powerful visual exorcism of repressed human needs; the shame we hold when we go physically and emotionally hungry, can lead to irrevocable loss.

Exercises

1. Out of all six Hungers, which are the ones you most identify as belonging to your mother and why?
2. Out of all six Hungers, which are the ones you most identify as belonging to your father and why?
3. Out of all six Hungers, which are the ones you most identify as belonging to you and why?

References

Berne, E. (1961). *Transactional Analysis in Psychotherapy: A Systematic Individual and Social Psychiatry*. New York: Grove Press.

Kolk, S. M and Rakic, P (2021). Development of prefrontal cortex. Available at: https://www.nature.com/articles/s41386-021-01137-9 (accessed 15 January 2024).

Pradhan, G., Samson, S.L., Sun, Y. (2013). Ghrelin: much more than a hunger hormone. Available at: https://pmc.ncbi.nlm.nih.gov/articles/PMC4049314 (accessed 5 January 2024).

6

The Drama Triangle and *Hillbilly Elegy*

Theory: The Drama Triangle

The psychological theory of assuming a certain position, either persecutor, victim or rescuer and being confined to repeating patterns of dysfunctional behaviour (Karpman 1968).

Movie: *Hillbilly Elegy (2020)*

A brilliant law student finds himself conflicted. Does he return home where his mother Bev has just overdosed on heroin and leave his career-defining dinner only to risk being drawn back into old patterns of family dysfunction? Based on a memoir by JD Vance (at the time of writing, Vice President of the United States) from Ohio, this is a story about his rough start and troubled teen years before his arrival at the climactic final interview for a prestigious law firm. We learn how JD escapes a life that to many might seem entirely inescapable. With histories of domestic violence and skating perilously close to foster care, he is saved by his grandmother, Mamaw, and his sister, Lindsey, as his emotionally unpredictable mother, Bev, struggles with drugs, in and out of one short-lived relationship/marriage after another. The story's plot is the single fact that JD ends a cycle of perpetuating behaviours that have spanned across generations, and by doing this, he introduces something different into the family lineage.

What We're Doing

In this chapter, we will be looking at the drama triangle when applied to the Vance family in the movie *Hillbilly Elegy*. As we learn about the model, we will use it to understand and explore relationships of an inter-generational nature and also between the generations of this family. Using my own experience in training, I invite you to consider how the theory may relate to your life.

One storm cloud gathered Sunday, 18 would-be counsellors met for process group. We were entirely unaware of the drama that was to unfold and assumed that the air of something imminent must surely be the fury of the impending storm in the sky. People gather in the kind of slow body motion you might expect on an early Sunday morning. Making cups of tea and coffee was a ritual, helping both to open the eyes and obfuscate the trepidation of this strange class timetabled on the curriculum with no obvious goal or objective. As the hands of the clock edged slowly towards 9, we began the solemn walk to the gallows, finding our seats. This was the part of the weekend where we were not taught but instead sat leaderless for three hours, with no set agenda, nothing to do other than arrive and survive. Bella, our tutor, sat slightly off to the side trying to make herself as innocuous as a pot plant. This was the time we sat with ourselves, and it wasn't that we weren't allowed to talk, necessarily, but with no brief to follow and nobody in charge, it just happened that nobody did. In the beginning anyway. Anticipatory anxiety hung like stalactites in the air and the pretty Victorian house began to morph into a dimly lit cave with low, oppressive ceilings. It felt like nothing I'd ever done before and at the same time like something I'd always wanted to do but not known why.

Choosing where to sit on a Sunday morning had a different feel – a particular flavour of daunting. With apparently more at stake without our tutor Bella as a buffer, who you sat next to felt even more important than in a normal class. Silence became many things – uncomfortable and comforting, interminable and fleeting, curious and boring. It enveloped each one of us as individuals whilst also cocooning us as a group. Despite having interacted with each other for the whole Saturday, somehow we began Sunday as strangers once again. It was as if we had been shrunk into tiny humans, inspecting ourselves from inside a petri dish and here, under these laboratory conditions of leaderlessness, we were set to learn something about ourselves that would enable us to better understand our dysfunction with the outside world. In that moment, there was something crucial in the order of things which stated that before we can look at the dysfunction rife 'out there' we must locate the dysfunction present 'in here.'

And this is where the movie begins. The film's opening sees JD's sister Lindsey plead for his return home, where the horror of JD's childhood screams to him. Home is not a place JD wants to return to. In fact, he has never worked harder for anything in his life at that point than to leave home and it is this hard work, this mental determination, resilience and resolve, that has him on the precipice of an outstanding opportunity that could change his life. As JD returns to Middletown, Ohio, all we can do is watch as the tragedy of generational trauma repeats itself and our protagonist does what is expected of him but not what he wants. We watch the pain felt by all the characters and how they inflict said pain between three generations of family members. In the flashbacks into JD's childhood, it becomes tragically clear how the choices and limitations of one generation directly impact the next.

Without a designated person in charge, I feel a growing unease and wonder why it is that groups need a leader. Structure seems an obvious reason to provide a purpose for our time. In this way, we know what is happening. We are aware of the story and know what to tell ourselves. The absence of such structure creates confusion around knowing exactly what we are meant to be doing together. Bubbles of tension rise and pop in my stomach. Nobody speaks. Face twitching and leg adjustments are contagious. Eyes flicker across the room, then to the ground. What else can the presence of a leader do? Alleviate the possibility of anarchy? Create a power structure where individuals may need to submit their will to the collective? Avoid any chance for self-reflection?

A young man, Malechai, sat diagonally opposite me, speaks with a furrowed brow, breaking the reverie. Hearing his voice from the depths of the quiet felt oddly jarring and yet, I am grateful. The sound of sound. It feels like it comes from the bowels of somewhere. One lone voice but maybe speaking for all of us.

Malechai says he is upset because of an interaction he has had earlier with Wednesday. All heads angle forward as if on cranes zooming in towards Wednesday. What had happened? Did she know this was coming? Had she also been upset by said interaction? Under scrutiny, Wednesday's features appear devoid of recognition and she appears as clueless as the rest of us. I notice we are all poised, just like Wednesday, to hear what Malechai is going to say as it slowly dawns on us that Wednesday could be any one of us – that Malechai could just as easily be outraged at something Bob had said or even me and that we were all characters in this story with no idea as yet which role we were to play. In fact, for the next three hours, any one of us could say anything to anyone in this strange and unstructured manner, and it may even be what we were being encouraged to do.

Malechai tells the group that he felt attacked by Wednesday. Attacked? I feel myself looking at the group as if on the outside – observing them from above, an aerial view, anything to avoid being close up where tensions feel unpredictable. How? When? Are there scars? Witnesses? I begin to have an awareness of my own assumptions and wonder why I have so quickly moved to needing to figure things out. Perhaps it is to ease my unease. I use the little information I have to solve the mystery – I know that Malechai and Wednesday are friends and travel to school together. I suppose I expected that this allegiance must provide safety and I wonder if

Wednesday felt the same way. Malechai begins to reveal that he has worked hard to learn English and though he has had to endure shaming for his accent many times before, he did not expect to experience it here, a place he thought he would feel safe.

In *Hillbilly Elegy*, JD expected to feel safe in his family but he soon came to understand that it was in his family that he was first able to experience and become part of unsettling dynamics with anyone at any time. Does this process group reenact our original family? Does every group? JD desperately confesses to a policeman that his mother is in fact trying to kill him and this is why he has sought refuge in the house of a stranger. The policeman says to a young JD, '*Son, this may be normal in your family but it's not right.*'

Wednesday is now visibly aghast and says she cannot remember shaming Malechai in any way and that when she had corrected his English, she had not meant to attack Malechai but to illuminate/help Malechai. If this was how he felt, she asks, why had he not mentioned it to her? Immediately, I am aware that what constitutes an attack for Malechai registers as confusion for Wednesday.

My body feels like the metal ball in a pinball machine and Malechai and Wednesday are the flippers. I ping between them, first to total appreciation of Malechai's outrage and then flipped back to complete understanding of Wednesday's shock. It's mere moments before I am flipped again, now able to relate to Malechai's upset, only to just as suddenly empathise with Wednesday's bewilderment. As Malechai and Wednesday talk about a shared reality via different filters of experience, I see the individuals in the group are also pinball machines, their flippers working in the same way as mine. Malechai is most distressed and his anger pushes hot tears from his eyes but as he hurls words of blame in Wednesday's general direction, I feel uncertain whether Wednesday even has the capacity at this point in the course to comprehend what is happening. It starts to feel that maybe Malechai's hurts are not from Wednesday and originate instead from something older, a piece of something from another story and another time that has survived inside him. Something he may have brought with him. As I start to get in touch with my own sense of fear, I begin to see what is driving Wednesday to withdraw. I wonder if she has anger, too. The drama in *Hillbilly Elegy* feels equally reactive, explosive, unclear as to who is really at fault and an overwhelming sense of being trapped in a family who are bound to specific ways of behaving. JD is abused by his mother but also seeks her love. He is not only manipulated by his grandma but also protected by her. He is understood by his sister but also guilted by her. The roles feel unstable and unreliable. Necessary and needed. The only consistent thing in JD's life is the drama.

Bella tries to interject over Malechai's breaking sobs, proceeding to list all the reasons Malechai should value himself as a person, all the positive qualities Malechai has to offer which she herself could see in him. Like dominoes, people fall into line, following Bella's lead and one by one they too offer Malechai all the reasons they value him. As Bella spoke, I could feel her words softening all the hard edges of the morning, the contours of Malechai's jawline relaxing as Bella's voice began to parentally repair the rupture, soothing Malechai from his attack. A rupture for Malechai but also for the group and one which had appeared as sudden and deep as a fissure through a rock. Though the group and Malechai seemed to have benefited from Bella's gentle parenting, I noticed Wednesday was experiencing something else. Bella had rescued Malechai, leaving Wednesday with a feeling of rejection. Why had no one thought to rescue her? I sit with my shame, grateful that Malechai is not having this conversation with me and also full of shame that my gratitude for my own safety does nothing to help Wednesday.

Trapped in my own silence, I wonder what inhibits us and what aids us to find our voice, and if announcing his feelings in front of a group of strangers had felt easier for Malechai than telling Wednesday himself. If it had even provided some other comfort. A group hug? A public hanging? I wondered how Malechai might hold and carry around his pain of being shamed for his accent. And perhaps the fact that Wednesday and Malechai had formed a friendship so early on is what had enabled Malechai to have the trust in the first place and get in touch with his shame. I wondered why Wednesday became visibly smaller as Malechai spoke and could not verbally communicate the shock in her eyebrows or anger in her crossed arms and what she might have needed in that moment to relax her frosted smile? I wondered also if, as a tutor, Bella had felt the need to calm her new recruits before the battle scars of the experiential process group became too deep and if in saving Malechai, she was trying to save herself as well, save the class, and save the course.

What was clear was the confusion in who appeared to be persecuting who, who was rescuing who, and that everybody felt as though they could be a victim. It was the same in *Hillbilly Elegy*. JD, Bev and Mamaw constantly moved positions on the drama triangle (Figure 6.1). As the course progressed, the reality of our Sunday process group emerged. The bonds we formed on Saturday were tested at random on Sunday. It was like our stories, our histories and our experiences could and most probably would meet together in this human centrifuge called process group and what was spat out could and most probably would be emotional, unpredictable and triggering for us all, but that also, and perhaps most shocking, would look completely different to each one of us. That somehow we could all behave as and be perceived as the persecutor, feel like the victim and also have the inclination to rescue each other and the need to be rescued.

The drama triangle posits that in families or groups – families being our first ever group experience – we gravitate to a position on the triangle. The position we choose depends on what we might emotionally require from the situation, whether other positions are already taken, as well as what position sits most comfortably within our personality. We might have a default position which usually feels more acceptable than the other two; however,

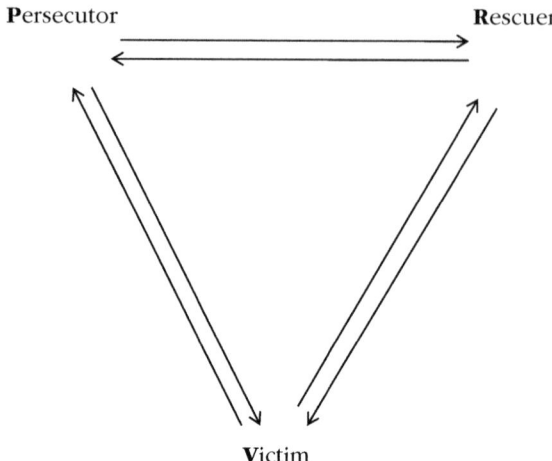

Fig. 6.1   The Drama Triangle. Source: Karpman (1968)/Stephen B. Karpman

when a situation threatens to expose vulnerable parts of ourselves, we swap momentarily to another. This switch alleviates anxiety by providing a sense of illusory strength or indeed relief in that moment. We quickly fall back into our old position once the explosion/exposure is over. It is the switching that helps perpetuate the cycles through the generations and keeps both hope and confusion alive.

The common denominator through the positions is power. The persecutor uses/abuses power by dominating the others with their own power. The victim gives their power away, feeling powerless. The rescuer uses their power to behave in ways that appear helpful but take power away from the others, where they might make decisions for themselves.

JD suffered childhood emotional neglect (Chapter 18) despite his family trying their best to raise him. As a child, he had no choice but to try to cope with the emotional instability but as an adult, he managed to leave Ohio – an effort to leave the drama triangle and the psychological dysfunction that characterised his childhood. Mamaw and Bev's ancestors will have also moved through all three roles on the triangle. Even JD's sister Lindsey is in danger of repeating the pattern as we hear Mamaw say, '*JD's not your responsibility.*' Lindsey replies, '*Whose is he then?*' Mamaw recognises the errors of her parenting with Bev and encourages JD to break the cycle by going to college and not succumbing to the prolific drug exposure within his family and wider social environment.

In an early scene from childhood, which ironically begins with Bev attempting to make up for her bad behaviour, Bev is seen driving erratically, frightening a young JD who is begging his mother to slow the car down. A visibly angry and upset Bev says,

I could crash. I could crash this car and I could kill us and then you would know how lucky you are.

Persecutor?

It is easy for this comment to be understood on first reading as being made by someone occupying the persecutor position. A deeper under-standing would reveal that for Bev to feel like killing them both could be a viable solution, she must be in a lot of pain. She herself is feeling like a victim. She feels powerless, as she did as an abused child but now also as an adult suffering from drug addiction. Her life has felt more unfair than fair and she has felt victimised through birth and circumstance, assuming the victim position. A more extreme reading might be that for Bev to harm herself or another, she has occupied the rescuer position herself, believing she is saving herself and her son from the pain of having her as a mother and JD ending up as unhappy in his life as she is in hers.

When JD learns from Lindsey that Bev had suffered during difficult growing-up years with Mamaw and that Mamaw is now a better grand-mother than she ever was a mother to Bev, he is shocked. He was aware of his own frustrations but unaware that this was trauma that had been passed down through the generations and was not just intergenerational. Bev's father was abusive and would beat his wife, Mamaw, during the time Mamaw was raising Bev. Mamaw would then go on to emotionally abuse her daughter, Bev. Mamaw, herself a victim, would then go on to be Bev's persecutor.

The persecutor, victim and rescuer are so enmeshed in Mamaw, Lindsey and Bev that they almost finish each other's sentences. This is because of the ease with which we can occupy different positions on the triangle, especially within a family. We get caught up in the drama as a way to avoid dealing with our real pain and our real shame which is all about not feeling good enough and processing losses of love, childhood and safety. JD assumes Bev as the persecutor only to suddenly see her as the victim when he hears of her own suffering with Mamaw, a woman JD would describe as his rescuer. Bev says,

I could have done whatever I wanted but I didn't have somebody taking me to the library and telling me I could go to college and gonna help me pay for it.

Victim?

Though Bev is explaining an experience that has had her feel victimised, her tone and behaviour can be seen as persecutory as her words are accompanied by a specific behaviour; recklessly driving while her son screams for her to stop. As she speaks, she gives a voice to the absent rescuer – there was no one to help Bev. JD has no relationship with his father and has had many men paraded in front of him. We see how burdened Bev, JD and Lindsey have become as parentified children, with emotionally and physically absent parents they were required to parent themselves from an early age. Bev goes on to say,

> *What do you think I do it for – so that you and Lindsay will have everything I never had.*

Rescuer?

Bev makes clear here her intention to rescue her children and that the essence of what she is trying to do involves rescuing them from suffering. As the speedometer keeps climbing, JD becomes more and more terrified, and the irony is that he needs the eventual help of a stranger, the police and Mamaw to rescue him from his mother. Bev is getting more upset, recounting the past she regrets and the present she struggles with. She ignores her son's pleas, neglecting his fear and the worthy intentions of Bev's comment become frighteningly contradictory as she puts her foot down on the accelerator, heading into persecutory terrain and behaving as if she wants to kill them both. '*Everything I never had,*' illustrates her sense of victimhood as a motivating force as she moves between persecutor and rescuer. The movie brilliantly shows how blurry the lines become in a family, between the generations but also on a primal and internal level, between our own motivations.

Persecutor: JD, Mamaw, Lindsey, Bev
The person who uses a display of emotional power to discount the other.
Victim: JD, Mamaw, Lindsey, Bev
The person who feels powerless to make a different choice and discounts themselves.
Rescuer: JD, Mamaw, Lindsey, Bev
The person who discounts another's ability to empower themselves.

> MAMAW: *Everyone in this world is one of three kinds; a good terminator, a bad terminator and neutral.*
> JD: *You're the good terminator.*
> MAMAW: *Wasn't always. Had to learn.*

Mamaw's words illustrate how she is consciously becoming aware of the positions she has held on the drama triangle and that she is trying to come off the triangle by assuming no position at all. She raised Bev in an abusive household but stopped being the victim in her story to raise JD with an agency and a power she herself had not always had access to. Often, the rescuer is viewed by society as the better position, even the kinder position due to a belief that they are saving the victim. However, the victim will remain a victim unless they learn to rescue themselves, as echoed in JD's words at the end of *Hillbilly Elegy,* in how he managed to overcome his traumatic legacy:

> *Twice I've needed to be rescued. The first time it was Mamaw who saved me. The second it was what she taught me, that where we come from is who we are but we choose every day who we become.*

Exercises

1. Thinking about your first group experience (family) – which position on the drama triangle do you feel was your default position?
2. What do you think it was that made you choose that position and do you adopt that same position today?
3. Think about which relationships today feel as if they may have you and the other person on the drama triangle.

Reference

Karpman, S. (1968). Fairy tales and script drama analysis. *Transactional Analysis Bulletin* 7 (26): 39–43.

7

Drivers and *The Wizard of Oz*

Theory: Drivers

A psychological theory of five unconscious messages (Kahler 1975): Please Others, Hurry Up, Be Strong, Be Perfect, Try Hard (a sixth, Take It (Tudor 2008), came later) which drive, motivate and dictate our behaviour – these are Drivers that become embedded in our personality.

Movie: *The Wizard of Oz (1939)*

A little girl becomes concussed after a fall, drifting into an unconscious fantasy dream world where members of her family and home life morph into archetypal characters. Feeling a long way from home and frighteningly lost, Dorothy must embark on a quest involving many adversarial encounters before she can return home.

What We're Doing

In this chapter, we will be looking at Drivers when applied to the personalities of the five main characters of *The Wizard of Oz*. As we learn about the theory of Drivers, we will use it to understand and explore the motivations and behaviour, implicit and explicit, which play an important role in shaping each character's personality. Using my own experience in training, I invite you to consider how the theory may relate to your life.

Dorothy lives with her Aunty Em and Uncle Henry on a farm in Kansas. Her stern-looking neighbour, Almira Gulch, has been bitten by Dorothy's dog, Toto and, to Dorothy's horror, is all out to exact her punishment on the dog and its owner. Professor Marvel, a travelling charlatan, suggests to

Dorothy, who is planning to run away to save Toto, that she return to her family, who love her. Whilst Dorothy and Toto prepare to run away, a tornado hits their house and Dorothy is knocked unconscious. She and the audience seamlessly enter the dreamlike 'Munchkinland,' an unfamiliar place where Dorothy meets witches, a wizard, a scarecrow, a tin man and a lion, all representations of people in her real life. And all Dorothy really wants to do is go back home to Kansas.

I am thinking about home and what that is. Is it a place, a person, a feeling? This counselling course is starting to feel like all those things. Firstly, a place I visit regularly. Secondly, a place where there are people becoming familiar to me and thirdly, a place where the people in it are giving me a sense of feeling at home. I have made good friends with people who speak my language and in this group, I feel a peculiar sense of belonging. A quiet orchard with strange and mysterious low-hanging fruit.

Bella starts talking about counselling placements, about how important they are and that without a placement we cannot pass the course. As she speaks, the fruit in the orchard starts to shrivel. Tranquility is ruptured as something discordant builds. There is a collective shudder as a small self-created tornado of panic appears in the room and everyone is visibly anxious. Why do adults get feelings of excitement and nervous terror so confused?

We are told we will need a placement to accumulate the training hours required to pass the exam, 750 to be exact. My first thought is that this number seems excessive. Research confirms my assumption, as many other psychotherapy courses ask for significantly fewer hours; however, this is research I compile after the fact, and the course has already begun. Which brings me to my next point of awareness – it was my impulsive urgency, not a new impulsivity I might add, which compelled me to enrol in a course without doing any research in the first place. Truth be told, 750 hours in and of itself might not be too much as I have nothing to compare it to. What I do know is that I have to Hurry Up. The need to move fast drives me and it always has.

There and then, as Bella talks, I plan. We all knew there was a clinical hours requirement and yet reality has shocked us. How can we possibly secure a placement? What is to be made of the number of placements versus the larger number of psychotherapy trainees? That evening, I sat and faced the beast I'd locked in the basement: the course handbook. It growled at me and snapped at my heels with jaws salivating, but I kept my resolve and headed straight to the placements database page of the website. The first thing I learnt was that 750 hours was the number needed for a Master's. Phew! There was no way I was doing a Master's. A diploma, on the other hand, was 450 hours, which appeared possible. Plausible. Most of the organisations offering placements asked for a certain number of training hours to have been accrued already. All except one – a GP practice – and scanning through the applicant profile, I start to get excited. A little voice whispers to me, '*they won't like this*,' but I ignore her and drop an email to the course leader. Promptly, she emails back confirming there is no problem with me taking on this placement at this time. '*Happy now?*' I say to the little voice. She is quiet, but I can tell she is also unconvinced.

I prep for the interview, brimming with as much psychotherapeutic theory as I can contain. The interview for the voluntary placement lasted one hour with a panel of three senior therapists. Midway through, it dawned on me that they did not want to know everything I knew about Eric Berne, the father of Transactional Analysis or even Sigmund Freud, the father of Psychoanalysis, but the person they did want to know about was me. My life, me as a person, the emotional experiences which had shaped me and how I had responded to them and reflected upon them, my thoughts on the purpose of therapy and how I planned on sitting with a client. I wondered if perhaps they were also asking how I sit with myself in life. A few days after the interview, the practice contacted me and offered me the placement. I was over the moon.

I had been working in the GP practice for about two months, and loving every minute of it, when Bella made a curious comment. During exercises known as triads, where groups of three students assume the role of therapist, client and observer, Bella mentioned how unfamiliar we will all be with this practice as none of us is in a placement as yet. A stone drops all the way to the bottom of the pond. I tell Bella I have been in a placement for two months now. I watched the slow spread of shock and confusion across her cheekbones. Dutifully, she tells me she must alert the course leader. Calling for reinforcements from higher up? Never a good sign, I think to myself.

The course leader writes to me, again, firmly, '*no students are allowed to undertake placements in year one*.' I am told I must leave the GP practice. I am devastated, sad and angry. My two-month career as a trainee psychotherapist is over and not only has the course leader not commented on why she might have said yes the first time but no the second, but I cannot make sense of it. Why would you want to make securing a placement harder when, in a few months, we will have to find one anyway? The word 'discretionary' lurks in the back shadows of the handbook. Why can I not be party to your discretion? What's wrong with me? I am asked to come in for a meeting. '*Do I have a problem with authority?*' she asks. This has got to be a trick question. 'No,' I say. A big, fat lie. Authority slows me down. She knows it and I know it. And this rule, this fly in the ointment, this obstacle in my way, only serves to increase my need to Hurry Up.

We can all make choices. We can all change our destiny. We all have the capacity to think. These are the three philosophical assumptions of Transactional Analysis (Berne 1961). But why do we make the choices we do? Why do some people hurry and some do not; some challenge authority and some do not. How do we think and make choices in a way that allows us to reach our highest potential? Drivers change our perspective, our priorities and our permissions. As children, we look for permission from our caregivers and other adults to do most things. Permission to take the last piece of cake. Permission to go outside and play. Permission to say how we feel. Permission to feel safe. As our selection of Drivers are early decision choices, they relate directly to a sense of permission. Children need to be safe and to feel safe. How safe we feel is directly wired into our nervous system. Therefore, we choose Drivers which allow us to feel safe in our environment, to feel OK.

When Dorothy woke up in Kansas, she was shocked to learn that her house had been picked up by the tornado and landed on the Wicked Witch of the East, killing her. Despite the jubilation of the citizens of Munchkinland, now freed from the tyranny of the evil witch (of which nothing is left but two legs in stripy tights and ruby slippers), Dorothy is more traumatised by the witch's raging sister, the Wicked Witch of the West. Lost and alone, away from her family and all she knows, Dorothy has done a terrible thing and is scared. To cope, she defaults to her Driver: I need to Hurry Up and get the hell out of Oz.

Drivers are our chosen vehicle in which we move through the world to get our needs met. They are behaviours we have learnt at a young age to enable us to survive our environment. They are absorbed through non-verbal psychological messaging which we intuit as children and absorb. We also gain information based on verbal messages that let us know which behaviours are permissible and which are not. In some families, we are encouraged to move quickly, learn fast and get things done. An emphasis on achieving in a results-focussed manner. Living on a farm, Dorothy was used to having to do a lot, quickly. When we are young, we tell ourselves the stories that allow us to best survive and how the story is told depends on our perspective. But there are many ways to tell a story, even to ourselves about ourselves as we can see in this luculent illustration of a television listing.

that order.

The Wizard of Oz. (8-10 p.m., TCM) — Transported to a surreal landscape, a young girl kills the first person she meets and then teams up with three strangers to kill again.

Inquirer Television Writer Lee Winfrey

Drivers are neither good nor bad, but understanding our Drivers allows us to know whether the Drivers we relied upon as children are the Drivers we consciously want to use for the rest of our lives and in every situation. The diagnosis of a client's Drivers is best achieved using the four methods of Transactional Analysis diagnosis: social, behavioural, historical and phenomenological (Tudor and Widdowson 2008). There is often one dominating Driver, as well as another, less obvious secondary Driver. Some people have two Drivers equally and then there are cases where three Drivers seem to present. Difficulty in identifying Drivers can also reveal something about a person and a sense of their fragmentation and trauma.

Hurry Up

'*Now I'll never get home,*' wails a despairing Dorothy, desperate to return home to Kansas from the magical land of Oz. '*All in good time, my little pretty,*' replies the Wicked Witch to Dorothy. That's the worst thing someone with a Hurry Up Driver wants to hear. I don't have enough time, thinks Dorothy. Dorothy interrupts others, speaks incredibly fast, connecting sentences without pauses and taps her feet (her heels, to be exact). Being stranded in Oz has her in a state of agitation which feels unbearable. Why does the present seem so difficult to tolerate and what exactly is the need for the hurry? Once we have hurried up and gotten to where we need to be, can we stop and pause or will we still find something we must hurry towards? Are we running towards something or away from something? Dorothy tries to avoid having to feel the fear of being scared, lost and all alone and the even deeper pain of the loss of her family.

I'll be OK if I hurry up and get home to Kansas.

Be Perfect

Tin Man stands straight and tall with shiny, unblemished metal – albeit on the verge of rust. '*You're perfect now,*' says Dorothy, but Tin Man does not feel perfect – he wishes to be human. A sober kind of guy, sombre with tightly held lips. '*Hearts will never be practical until they can be made unbreakable,*' the Wizard tells him, warning Tin Man of the imperfections of being human. '*I still want one,*' says Tin Man.

'*You people with hearts have something to guide you and need never do wrong; but I have no heart and so must be very careful.*' Tin Man appears immaculate, flawless with a steely expression. Be Perfect types wear external signs of perfection as a protective mask so people, and they themselves, are distracted from the pain of feeling loss. They might need to be the perfect friend or the perfect parent or the perfect employee or all three. *'I'll be OK once . . .'* they say to themselves.

Tin Man's belief is that once he gets a heart, all his problems will be solved. He doesn't understand that he must face all the imperfections in himself rather than look for external solutions – like a human heart. He must grieve the loss of his heart, like a real human.

I'll be OK, if I achieve human perfection and get a heart.

Try Hard

Lion tries valiantly to appear courageous, but his scrunched-up brow and wrinkled old man face give him away. He is terrified all the time but being the supposed king of the jungle means he must hide his fear. His voice swallows inside his throat. *'I even scare myself,'* Lion says. He puts off what he needs to do – *'talk me out of it,'* he tells Tin Man and Scarecrow. *'Victim of disorganised thinking,'* says the Wizard. Lion tries hard to distract himself from the fear of failure in his own abilities. He battles internally with the shame of finding things difficult. The things he struggles with plague his mind and he finds it hard to be vulnerable for fear of feeling shame. If Lion were to stop trying so hard, he would need to grieve the loss of connection to the idea of what he thinks a lion should be in this world.

I'll be OK, if I try hard to be brave.

Take It

Scarecrow stands pointing, his hands held out. *'I'm not afraid of anything. I'll do anything to get a brain.'* *'I got a plan to get us in there,'* he tells Lion. The strength of Scarecrow's belief that he needs a brain is so strong that he is empowered to face up to the Wicked Witch and do whatever he needs to do to be OK. He'll take it any way he can and all his energy is driven towards what he believes he must have to be OK in the world. But when Dorothy says, *'I'm going to miss you the most,'* he is silent, non-relational. It is easier to take it because then he is doing and avoiding the difficulty in relating to others with honesty. His brain is the focus rather than the emotional connection of having a friend and the emotional pain of losing her. Desperate to seem together and in control, he tries to avoid grieving the loss of what he does not have.

I'll be OK, if I can only take a brain.

Be Strong

'*These things must be done delicately or you hurt the spell*.' The Wicked Witch uses distancing language to avoid talking about herself and the pain of losing her sister, the Witch of the East. '*Look what you've done*,' she says, seeing Dorothy as responsible for all her uncomfortable feelings. Mounting her broom, she assumes a rigid posture, a hardness to her face and tone of voice. She speaks dismissively to her monkey minions. Maintaining a cold exterior, she keeps herself from getting close to others to protect herself from her deepest fear – revealing her vulnerability. She believes that if she is strong, she will not be touched by her grief and the loss of her sister, but underneath, she is much less scary than she can ever let on. She fears that her vulnerability will be what can leave her most exposed and at risk of harm as at her core, she is so soft she could melt.

I'll be OK, if I kill Dorothy.

Please Others

'*Please don't cry anymore, I'll get you into the Wizard somehow*,' the Wizard himself says to Dorothy. The Wizard has created a false persona to give the impression to the people of Oz that he has power. He knows this power pleases them and this validation helps him avoid the pain of how powerless he really feels. His constant amenable demeanour elicits gratitude from others, throwing them off the scent of the Wizard's own insecurities. The Wizard does not feel good enough, so he creates a booming voice and omniscient presence. When exposed as a fraud – '*I'm a humbug*,' he says, this time without a smile – he is forced to accept his own limitations and capabilities. '*The only way to get Dorothy back to Kansas is to take her there myself*.' He believes that if he is pleasing, he can avoid the loss of how he imagined things would be in his life, and the shame of confronting his true lack of self-worth and exposing this to others.

I'll be OK, if I please everyone by pretending to be a powerful Wizard.

After many years of using survival techniques created by our very young Child parts, not yet emotionally developed or even fully formed, if we look closely enough, we can identify repetitive cycles in our life, patterns of behaviour or experiences that feel familiar. These trusted Drivers, which have served us so well, may no longer work in our favour and may, in some cases, be creating more problems for us.

We see Dorothy hurry with every fibre of her being in an effort to get back to Kansas and to her family. The Wizard, being just a man and not *'really great and powerful,'* was unable to take her to Kansas himself. When Dorothy stopped trying to get somewhere else, she found she was exactly where she needed to be and had been there all along. At the end of the movie, Glinda, the Good Witch, tells her, *'You don't need to be helped any longer, you've always had the power.'* Dorothy had to find out for herself that she did not need her Hurry Up Driver as much as she thought and that when she stopped hurrying, she discovered two things: that she was at home all along and just having a dream, and that home was a return to herself – to the self. Dorothy discovers she is inherently OK and good enough without doing anything at all.

Exercises

1. Identify which Driver/s you have.
2. Which Driver/s do you feel you have a strong reaction to and why? Might they remind you of someone?
3. Can you imagine any areas in your life where you would like to employ different Drivers? Maybe in a specific relationship.

References

Berne, E. (1961). *Transactional Analysis in Psychotherapy: A Systematic Individual and Social Psychiatry*. New York: Grove Press.

Kahler, T. (1975). Drivers: the key process of scripts. *Transactional Analysis Journal* 4 (1): 26–42.

Tudor, K. (2008) "Take It": A Sixth Driver. *Transactional Analysis Journal* 38: 43–57.

Tudor, K. and Widdowson, M. (2008). From client process to therapeutic relating: a critique of the process model and personality adaptation. *Transactional Analysis Journal* 38: 218–232.

8

Parentification and *Mermaids*

Theory: Parentification

A psychological theory where the child takes on the role of the parent or adult caregiver at an age which is developmentally inappropriate and creates emotional ramifications in later years/adulthood (Boszormenyi-Nagy and Spark 1973).

Movie: *Mermaids (1990)*

Mermaids, based on the novel by Patty Dann, begins with Charlotte's 15-year-old voice introducing her sister, 9-year-old Kate, who she adores, and her mother, Rachel, who Charlotte refers to as Mrs. Flax. Charlotte's father is not around. The film uses comedy to gently explore Charlotte and Mrs. Flax's complicated relationship and how Mrs. Flax relies on Charlotte to help her parent her sister Kate. In prayer, Charlotte asks God to help her stop lying all the time, an example of which is telling her date that Mrs. Flax is '*a wonderful mothe*r.' When Mrs. Flax begins dating, she begins to see her parenting through the eyes of her boyfriend Lou and is forced to confront some difficult truths.

What We're Doing

In this chapter, we will be looking at Parentification and the impact of this role reversal on 15-year-old Charlotte in the movie *Mermaids*. As we learn about the consequences of Parentification, we will use it to understand and explore Charlotte's relationship to her mother and also her relationship to her emotional self. Using my own experience in training, I invite you to consider how the theory may relate to your life.

In class, we are asked to look around the room and find a person who reminds us of one of our parents or primary caregivers. This reminder can be anything: a tone of voice, an expression, a characteristic. The instruction sounds simple and there are smiles as we each embark on the exercise. Bella gives us 15 minutes – is that not too long? With each exercise we do, it feels more normal to sit with a group of strangers and contemplate my internal world. One by one, we would announce the name of the person we had chosen and the reminder. Karen chose Noelle because of her buttercup-coloured curly hair. She said her mother's was the same and she always thought it was so pretty. Looking around the room, there are 17 people to choose from, but I can't find anyone. Not an inflection, a single mannerism or even a hat. As the group started talking, I noticed how easily people spoke about parental reminders they liked or that felt good when they said them out loud. A little over half the class had spoken when a quiet descended. There were no more contributions to be offered that morning. However, just because no one was speaking didn't mean people had nothing to say.

In *Mermaids*, we are often treated to Charlotte's internal monologue. Thoughts she does not utter out loud, but is thinking all the time. Whilst Mrs. Flax is in the bathroom, Charlotte asks if she can talk to her but then proceeds to wait in silence on the other side of the shower curtain. We can hear Charlotte's worries and concerns, but she can't bring herself to tell Mrs. Flax. The thoughts in her head give us clues as to why. '*Finger food is all the woman cooks, anything more she says is too big a commitment.*' '*Mrs. Flax is dating her boss, that means we'll be moving soon.*' '*We've moved eighteen times. It gets easy to read the signs.*' When there are no party snacks provided, Charlotte is often told to take care of dinner for her and her sister. Charlotte senses her mother's avoidant relationship to commitment, and uses the name 'Mrs. Flax' to distance herself from her complex relationship with a mother who says she is her mother but does not behave like one. Charlotte's relationship with her mother dominates her world.

At the next coffee break, we mingle in the kitchen. Those who had already shared their cheery anecdotal reminders drifted together to the big table. The few who had not, myself included, seemed to have sought smaller and more solitary spaces. I need a spoon and walk over to the corner cupboard but feel resistance twinge in my body. As I near the cutlery drawer, I see Margaret leaning against the counter and I will need to ask her to move if I am to reach my spoon. That's when I noticed it. The disapproving tautness that pulled at the edges of her mouth like invisible stitches. That's when I saw the reminder of my mother. Seeing the disapproval in Margaret's face,

I was reminded of how important it was to please my mother if I was to avoid the feeling that there was something wrong with me.

The term Parentification first came to prominence through Minuchin et al., family therapists who noted differences between emotional and instrumental Parentification (Minuchin et al. 1967). Instrumental Parentification involves tasks and more observable responsibilities. Emotional Parentification involves the child responding to the emotional needs of the parent.

Likely Parentification Situations:
- When a child is asked to provide financial support to the parent or household.
- When a child needs to care for a parent suffering from mental illness.
- When a child needs to care for a parent suffering from a chronic physical illness.
- When a child is used as an emotional confidante or therapist, perhaps during a separation or after a divorce.
- When a child is given excessive details about their parents' marriage or another situation which has them worried and upset.
- When a parent tries to hurt themselves in front of a child.
- When a child is required to take on excessive sibling responsibilities: food, transportation, education and/or health.
- When a parent suffers from addiction.
- When a parent is too young or emotionally immature.
- When a parent is emotionally unavailable, rejecting and/or neglectful.
- When a parent is in a physically or emotionally abusive relationship.
- When the child is being sexually or emotionally abused.
- When a parent makes the child engage in criminal acts.
- When the child experiences the death of a parent or sibling.

I try to be charitable by taking care of Kate and not killing my mother.

Here we see Charlotte, and her Instrumental Parentification duties, taking care of Kate. We also see Charlotte's anger, an associated behaviour as a result of Emotional Parentification. Mrs. Flax struggles with the physical and emotional weight of being a single parent. Let's be clear, when we talk about a child being Parentified or a Parentified adult, we are not talking about the part of parenting which is necessary, which offers the opportunity to build important skills for a person's growth and maturity. We are talking about experiences which are not appropriate for a child, feelings that weigh them down and go on to inhibit them from leading functioning adult lives with a sense of well being. Emotional Parentification can often go unnoticed as its less overt nature makes it easier to normalise and thus ignore.

MRS. FLAX: *'How do i look?'*
CHARLOTTE: *'Like a woman about to go forth and sin,'*
MRS. FLAX: *'Oh good, exactly the look I was hoping for.'*

Mrs. Flax's sexual confidence is contrasted with her teenage daughter's prudishness. When Mrs. Flax starts to show a romantic interest in Lou, she knows he will be at the school and goes to see him under the guise of her daughter's education. *'You never came to parent teacher meetings before,'* says Charlotte. Charlotte can sense the falsehood and motivation in Mrs. Flax's behaviour, but is shut down as Mrs. Flax dismisses her protests.

How does a child become Parentified? When it is not safe for the child to act their age, they adapt themselves to compensate for what the parent is unable to do. Sometimes, Parentification can begin as something else. The parent is intending to offer seminal lessons of growth and resilience to the child, but this continues for too long and it becomes damaging. Parentification can be a process that lasts decades and this is another reason it can become normalised because when we do something every day, it becomes learnt behaviour, like brushing our teeth.

'I am not invisible,' screams Charlotte. Charlotte and Mrs. Flax are having an argument, which is actually unusual for them. Any anger is likely to be suppressed by a Parentified child, as there will be no space for the child's emotions. Any sadness they also learn to hide as both anger and sadness interrupt/challenge the parents' belief that the dynamic is normal/healthy. Any fear they learn to split off, or disassociate from. Years later, even after the child has physically moved away from the parent, the trauma remains. Emotional Parentification is much less easily identifiable than Instrumental Parentification, so we must pay more attention to the behaviours developed as a consequence of this invisible trauma. For example, addiction, emotional eating, mental illness and dysfunctional relationships and behaviour often go undiagnosed, but are related to the effects of being a Parentified child. It can be difficult for many adults to identify Parentification criteria they might not see as relevant to them.

When Charlotte runs away, she is befriended by a young family. Instantly, she regales them with story after story of the many hours she spends with her father and how happy they are together. Her ability to embellish, to lie, desperately wanting to feel something other than the pain that she is feeling is in stark contrast to her inability to speak her truth to Mrs. Flax as she recounts with euphoric detail the life she wishes she had. It is only when Lou, Mrs. Flax's boyfriend, arrives to collect her that the fantasy breaks. In that moment, he bears witness to the weight put on this child and how this extravagant fantasy keeps her safe. At the same time, Charlotte also bears witness to hearing her lie out loud, seen through the eyes of Lou, and the realisation that her fantasy no longer keeps her safe as she sits steeped in shame. We see Charlotte's face crumble as she is exposed.

Her body posture collapses and she is put in the back of the car and driven away like a criminal. Nothing she has said is true, simply stories about how she'd like to feel, and she is left with the shame of desperately wanting a better version of her family, a mother who feels like a mother. What has she done wrong? Nothing, but the child blames themselves.

Please God don't let me fall in love and let me do disgusting things.

Charlotte has shown an early interest in religion and looks to God for guidance in the absence of a guiding parent. Mrs. Flax makes little jibes, consistent microaggressions which equally shame and push her daughter into developing her sexual self, maybe even before she is ready. When the family meet Joseph, a 26-year-old young man who lives in the village, Mrs. Flax says, '*26 and cute as a button, too bad you're set on being a nun.*' After a party and an argument with Lou, Mrs. Flax kisses Joseph and Charlotte is furious. Charlotte fears her mother will take away the man she loves and, in order to embody sexual confidence the only way she knows how, she dresses up like her mother, determined to have sex with Joseph for the first time. Charlotte has been tasked yet again with looking after her sister while Mrs. Flax is at a party and while Charlotte and Joseph are having sex, Kate falls into the creek below and nearly drowns. Mrs. Flax is raging. '*What's your major – town tramp?*' she spits. The scene of Charlotte having sex (birth) is shot to include Kate nearly drowning (death) and illustrates the consequences of Parentification as it is inserted into the child. Something extreme and possibly irrevocable has happened on Charlotte's watch and Mrs. Flax blames Charlotte without taking responsibility for her own actions.

The Parentified child has all of the responsibility, but none of the power. Charlotte begs Mrs. Flax to talk to her. '*Yes, I made a mistake; yes, I'm really really sorry it was a big mistake, I know that. You make mistakes; you're always screwing up and we're always paying for it!*' Parentified children/adults hold a lot of guilt and receiving the silent treatment from a parent serves to intensify those emotions, leading to feelings of shame.

Another consequence of Parentification which shows up in later adult life, often presenting as innocuous, centres around an underlying feeling of sadness or emptiness. It could feel like an inability to find meaning in life – is anyone really interested in me anyway? Feelings stored in the body can manifest physically as depression or headaches, and yet there is still a belief that nothing is really wrong and that there is nothing to complain about. It can feel like going through the motions of life as if watching it from the outside, like an out-of-body experience. Or a sense of not being liked or being particularly important and perhaps a pattern of unfulfilling relationships, cut short.

Consequences of Parentification can also present as anger centering around an underlying feeling of unfairness. Despite the Parentified adult doing their very best to cope, deep down there is the knowledge that something wasn't right and they didn't get what they needed as a child. This situation could lead to becoming easily emotionally dysregulated, a feeling of being attacked or criticised, and feeling easily defensive. Stored bodily feelings can physically manifest as irritable bowel syndrome (IBS) and other gut issues, post-traumatic stress disorder (PTSD) and complex post-traumatic stress disorder (C-PTSD). Charlotte screams, '*I want to stay and finish high school.*' The child is having to teach the parent.

Many adults have never uttered the words they wanted to say at the time of Parentification to anyone, let alone their parents.

Unprocessed feelings can also present as anxiety centering around an underlying feeling of fear. The need to please others has been overdeveloped as a way of coping and feeling safe. It can feel scary if the Parentified adult is unable to please or fix. Children do what they can to control an unstable environment. When the Parentified adult loses their feeling of control, it can be anxiety-inducing. Doing for others now feels normal, but at what cost? For the young child's level of psychological maturity, it was the best way they found to adapt and cope. Feelings will have been stored unprocessed in the body and now the adult finds themselves socially anxious or, at the other extreme, wearing a mask so no one can see the pain that lies behind. There are a myriad of ways Parentification can impact the adult, including how we attach to others and shaping our personality.

A recurring story about Kate's birth is how Charlotte pretended that Kate was hers and tried to make her call her Mum. We can see that from an early age, Charlotte was obedient and has behaved in many ways as Kate's pseudo-mother, and it is only with Charlotte's help that Mrs. Flax was free to parent Kate in a different way than how she had parented Charlotte.

When Mrs. Flax sees Charlotte praying to Jesus, she rolls her eyes and reminds her that they are Jewish. Mrs. Flax's distinction is not only deliberately comedic but also ironic, as Parentification is religion blind and this is the real falseness that Mrs. Flax cannot see. Her daughter is praying for help and adjusting her religious point of contact is futile. Parentification is also colour blind and affects people of all different cultures. This is because it is a symptom of how difficult humans find living and the ways in which we use each other to cope. Parentification is a system of legacy and identifying Parentification is not about blaming previous generations, but it is about acknowledging that the mechanism they used to cope with their own pain is how the shame is passed on from parent to child. Being able to separate our true selves from our Parentified selves means we do not continue to pass dysfunctional patterns of behaviour down to future generations.

Exercises

1. Looking back, what would you say your parents found difficult about parenting?
2. Are there things you did for your parents you would not want to replicate with your own children and why?
3. If your younger self could tell you the things they found difficult in childhood, things they might feel years later should have been the job of a parent rather than their job, what would these things be?

References

Boszormenyi-Nagy, I. and Spark, G. (1973). *Invisible Loyalties: Reciprocity in Intergenerational Family Therapy*. Hagerstown, MD: Harper & Row.

Minuchin, S., Montalvo, B., Guerney Jr. B. G. et al. (1967). *Families of the Slums*. New York: Basic Books.

9

The Parent Ego State and *Rebecca*

Theory: The Parent Ego State

Imagine a mosaic. Now imagine this mosaic is inside you and it is made up of lots of different non-verbal and verbal messages, and pieces of information from a group of specific types of people. These people are parents, caregivers, aunts, uncles, older siblings and other family members, teachers and anyone else of an authoritative perspective. We also call this part the introjected parent. Introjection is the unconscious taking in of something external. The parent 'injects' the child with their values, beliefs and ideas and the child unconsciously takes these messages in and forms their own Parent ego state (Berne 1961).

Movie: *Rebecca (1940)*

Based on Daphne Du Maurier's eponymous novel, *Rebecca* is a gothic, romantic thriller directed by Alfred Hitchcock. It tells the story of Maxim de Winter, desperately haunted by the death of his late wife, Rebecca, and apparently broken-hearted. As he stands on the edge of a cliff contemplating ending his life, he is jolted from his suicidal ideation by a young woman. Finding himself both distracted and intrigued by the intrusion, Maxim embarks on a whirlwind romance. The woman, fiercely timid, delights Maxim with her ability to lay bare her love for him; someone who supports and comforts him no matter what, who nurtures and nourishes him. It is only once they are married that the young woman is given a name and even then, we still never find out her birth name but know her only as the second Mrs. de Winter. The drive to Manderlay, Maxim's family estate, is arresting, overwhelming and daunting. The new bride takes in the tree-lined canopy path as it undulates through the beautiful grounds, finally arriving upon the sprawling, anthropomorphic mansion where Rebecca's spirit lives on, immaculately preserved by Rebecca's sinister housekeeper, Mrs. Danvers. Neither Maxim nor the second Mrs. de

Winter can escape Manderlay's disturbing legacy as they are slowly tormented with ghosts of the past reaching into the present and threatening the new couple's future.

What We're Doing

In this chapter, we will be looking at the Parent ego state through the eyes of the movie's main character, the new Mrs. de Winter in the film *Rebecca*. As we learn more about the Parent part of our internal world, we will use it to understand and explore Mrs. de Winter's relationship to herself and to others. Using my own experience in training, I invite you to consider how the theory may relate to your life.

We are coming to the end of the first year and, in all honesty, I have surprised myself to have made it this far as the journey has not been an easy one. It is a requirement to be in personal therapy once a week and, though I have had therapy before, never has it felt so compulsory and so exhausting. This is in part because of the training. The theory we learn in class sort of comes alive when it touches our personal experiences and makes the therapy that much richer, that much harder. It is also in part because of the privilege of working with clients and hearing and feeling how much pain is being carried, how it can alienate us from others and ourselves, but also that this pain is universal and that we all have it and are impacted by it. Then there is the practical aspect of juggling training with all the other things at this stage of life. I have heard people say, or have said to myself, '*I hear my mother's voice in my head.*' We assume the parent knows what is in our best interests. We defer to our parents as wise beings with knowledge. Some of this deference is based on practicality – as babies, we need them to keep us safe, to feed us, to help us survive the hardships of being a vulnerable human in this world. My South Asian heritage offers another angle. A strong and established cultural parent which comes in the form of a group of traditions and histories to ensure things are done in a certain way. There are appropriate behaviours that an individual in a certain culture is expected to adhere to, and going against the culture has repercussions and ramifications. One of these expectations and behaviours is to listen to your elders. Do not question, they know best. Adhering to these rules, many of them unspoken, is important as it keeps an entire culture psychologically safe, fed, and able to survive.

So when my course leader tells me I have to give up my placement, I am confused. I need to listen to her. But this is the placement I was given after a successful three-person panel interview, the placement I have been doing for two months already and with great results. I don't understand the rationale in giving something up if I will imminently be required to find it again. Crawling towards me is a miscreant sensation. The uncomfortable sense that I do not feel this parental figure actually knows what's in my best interests. This puts me in a quandary. I hear voices in my head coming from my Parent ego state, voices I have heard spoken verbally and non-verbally my whole life. Voices not just from my parents. Voices that are so deeply part of my rhetoric and, dare I say it, personality, they sound as if they are all my own. Disquieted with what is happening in my mind, I divert – what do I feel in my body? My palms sweat – is this fear? My legs tremble – could this be anger? My heart sinks – I feel sadness.

Despite conditioning and what we think we know, our body feels first. The thinking is secondary. Thinking is not our first movement, but depending on our early messaging, our environment and inherited genetic trauma, we may suppress or repress certain feelings and learn to turn off our relationship with the physical body. We therefore come to rely on and, in some cases, develop an over-reliance on our thoughts and, predominantly, our Parent ego state.

Rebecca's ghost is omniscient, to the point that when a newly married Mrs. de Winter answers the phone, instead of announcing herself as Maxim's new wife, she effectively kills herself, '*Mrs de Winter?*' *Oh I'm afraid you've made a mistake, Mrs de Winter's been dead for over a year.*' This example, and the absence of a first name, show us how the new Mrs. de Winter struggles to take up space. Rebecca functions as a parental figure, loud and severe, enforcing parental messages of ownership and dominance. Mrs. Danvers hovers over Rebecca's things macabrely preserved in Manderlay and stalks the new Mrs. de Winter from one dimly lit corridor to another. She frightens the poor woman, leading to her skittishly skulking around Manderlay trying to ignore the abundance of Rebecca's monogrammed memorabilia and functioning mostly from her Child ego state. Apologising all the time, looking down at the floor when spoken to, her back against the wall, literally, trying to minimise her needs and shrink her physical body.

'*Can't be too careful with children,*' Maxim says to Mrs. de Winter, offering a raincoat. Later, inquiring into Mrs. de Winter's whereabouts Maxim's sister Beatrice asks, '*Where's the child?*' Despite being able to offer Maxim a Nurturing Parent experience where he can feel lovable, she is unable to offer the same to herself over the deafening critical voices of Rebecca's ghost. But when a stormy night washes an old boat onto the shore and Rebecca's actual body is found to be contained inside the hull, everything changes. The woman falsely identified and lying in the family crypt is not Rebecca, as most people believed and our heroine suddenly experiences a dramatic change in her sense of self on hearing this news. Rebecca's foreboding presence from the grave had amalgamated with other critical and belittling voices already held in Mrs. de Winter's Parent ego state. In fact, when Maxim first meets her, she is the companion of an obnoxious woman, Mrs. Van Hopper, who belittles and insults her. Mrs. Van Hopper is another critical voice that merges with other already established messages of low self-worth established in her Parent ego state. The discovery of Rebecca's body allows Mrs. de Winter to get in touch with her own body, and other parts of herself, like her Adult ego state. She finds strength in the new realisation that Rebecca does not reign from the sovereignty of the family crypt but lies perished and rotting in the hold of a boat. She is able to quieten her Critical Parent and moves from living in a world dominated by her shy, insecure Child to one where her decisive, rational Adult comes to the fore. '*I am Mrs. de Winter now,*' she says with certainty and some defiance to a shocked Mrs. Danvers.

'*He never talks about it, of course, but he's a broken man.*' '*They say he simply adored her.*' '*I suppose he just can't get over his wife's death.*' People are right to appreciate Maxim's pain, but not for the reasons they might suppose. '*You thought I loved Rebecca? You thought that? I hated her,*' he exclaims to Mrs. de Winter the night they find Rebecca's body. Maxim confesses that his marriage to Rebecca was a lie. Four days after their nuptials, Rebecca revealed she was having an affair with her cousin, intending to have her cousin's baby and have him inherit Maxim's wealth. '*I never had a moment's happiness,*' he says. Maxim admits to being '*conscious of the family honour,*' and now regrets '*accepting her dirty bargain.*' Maxim's cultural script (Chapter 14) is loud. He feared scandal and family dishonour, a common Parent ego state message, feeling at the time that there was no other option but to comply.

Thinking about my own Parent ego state, I can relate to Maxim's situation and my internal monologue comes through:

> *The head of school is cross – don't make her more cross.*
> *You have to listen, she's your superior.*
> *You have no option but to comply.*

I feel trapped. I believed in the school and had trusted that it would see the best in me. I arrive at my therapist's house dejected and disillusioned. This relationship between me and my college is not what I thought it would be. My therapist listens to my sadness, my anger and my fear. She is quiet, patient and thoughtful.

Maxim buries his uncomfortable memories. He refuses to talk about things, preferring to describe himself as having funny moods or a bit of a temper. He says he doesn't want to even think about it, but suppressing his feelings does not prevent Rebecca's messages from becoming part of his Parent ego state and affecting his decisions, his behaviour and his happiness. They collide with messages that are already there, like suffering in silence for fear of family dishonour. Maxim confides,

It's all over now. The thing's happened. The thing I've dreaded day after day,
night after night.
Happiness is something I know nothing about.
If you had my memories, you wouldn't go there or talk about it or even think
about it.

When he meets Mrs. de Winter, her love feels so alien from anything he has ever known before. The pure and unconditional way she loves him and stands by him allows Maxim to have a different experience and his relationship with Mrs. de Winter starts to integrate into and reshape Maxim's Parent ego state. Messages of love and acceptance start to balance more critical messages of worthlessness and powerlessness, and develop an internal Nurturing Parent. Though our Parent ego states begin forming as soon as we are born, they are not static states. They are live inner spaces of our emotional internal world which change, need updating and modification as we continue living and experiencing. Have you ever found yourself saying, '*this isn't like me, I've never been like this before.*' It might be that we are reacting to a situation which did not happen in our childhood, but happened for the first time in our later life, a later trauma, like Maxim's acrimonious marriage to Rebecca, but we are using unconscious parts of ourselves that we are unaware of, which are from our childhood, to survive the later trauma.

We can also find ourselves saying, '*my parents weren't like this.*' It's possible we might be reacting to something in our childhood which has been internalised in such a way that it appears to be unrelated to our parents' characteristics or behaviour. For example, Maxim may not have ever seen his parents troubled by upholding the family honour, because the business of maintaining it was so imperative and non-negotiable, it did not even warrant being talked about. Maxim would have internalised the message around the family honour and when Rebecca proposed a marriage in name only, a heinous idea for Maxim for multiple reasons, not least because his heart and trust were broken, he would have felt compelled to uphold the family honour, whatever the cost and not knowing the cost. Thus, Maxim might see himself as being troubled by the family honour, when his parents were not.

Sometimes, our Parent ego state can be so controlling, an overdeveloped Critical Parent, that we look for external sources of validation to meet our emotional needs. This is until we can internalise new messages from a Nurturing Parent and balance things out. The movie is littered with Rebecca's initial 'R' and the frequent ellipses and faux pas made by other characters about Rebecca, '*Mrs. de Winter. . .I mean the late Mrs. de Winter,*' illustrate the pervasiveness of the Parent ego state. When we have a rogue Parent ego state running riot, becoming overly critical, we can have anger outbursts and fly off the handle, as Maxim does, or a shutdown response from sadness or fear, like Mrs. de Winter. Sometimes a controlling

Parent ego state can lead to dissociation, even if we can't remember why and perhaps have good relationships with our parents in the here and now. The night Rebecca's body is discovered, Mrs. de Winter finds a disassociated Maxim sitting like a small child, a faraway look in his eyes, his memory impacted.

I break away from my reverie, hearing my therapist call my name. She may have been calling it a few times but I didn't hear, lost in thought. It felt so sad not to be seen by the course leader; even sadder that it felt like there was no one to champion me. I was disconnected from where I was – in the mustard-cushioned chair with the wooden armrests. '*Have you thought about moving to another training school?*' my therapist asks, calmly. Excuse me? Is this some kind of joke? After one year, is she seriously suggesting I change school? I can't do that. I feel myself come back into my body. At that moment, I am no longer trapped. I have options, choices. It feels weird, scary. Unfamiliar. Wrong, even. Can I do this? I make a call and a week later, I have a telephone interview with a new school. I tell the new school's head about my placement. My voice lowers as I am expecting the gavel of bad behaviour to be brought down. It doesn't happen. Not only that, but she is interested in my work at the surgery and wants to know all about it! She thinks it is a good idea to have already begun collecting my client hours. I cannot believe what I am hearing – the extreme difference in the two schools. How Maxim must have felt the extreme difference between his two wives, the critical wife and the nurturing wife. I feel a sense of elation that I cannot quite believe.

'*None of us want to live in the past, Maxim least of all. It's up to you you know to lead us away from it,*' says Frank, Maxim's secretary, to Mrs. de Winter. Frank describes the way the Critical Parent can keep us stuck and bound to a past that no longer serves us. In contrast, Mrs. Danvers says, '*Nothing has been altered since that last night.*' Mrs. Danvers herself is stuck, bound by her grief with no access to her own Adult ego state. Rebecca's ghost held everyone trapped and it was only with the new messages brought by the second Mrs. de Winter that her ghost could be laid to rest and everyone could be free from the past to live in the present. Everyone except for Mrs. Danvers.

'*Rebecca's dead, that's what you've got to remember, she can't hurt you anymore,*' Mrs. de Winter says to Maxim. Mrs. de Winter tried hard to be as 'good' as Rebecca but, in reality, Rebecca was never that good. This is an irony epitomised in the false and heightened Parent ego state. Critical messages can often be distorted, and approval sought out from sources less qualified than they might appear, to the Child ego state or even from that of a confused/contaminated Adult ego state.

I am sad to leave my friends. I am scared to move schools. I am worried that it may be the wrong decision. My Parent ego state says I cannot disagree with my elders and I must not take up too much space. My therapist has modelled new parental messages for me and injected my Parent ego state with messages that are shifting the balance between the Critical Parent and the Nurturing Parent. Updating my core beliefs feels emotional and hard. I remember certain experiences I had in childhood. There is guilt and fear. There is anger towards my parents. There is sadness when I allow myself to feel the feelings from my childhood that I locked away, and sadness when I look at certain behaviours that have arisen as a result in adulthood. There is shame. That somehow I have not been enough.

The opening line of *Rebecca*, and one of its most famous, is by Mrs. de Winter, '*Last night I dreamt I went to Manderlay again.*' In my dreams, I disagree with those in authority, I make decisions for myself and I know in my heart it is okay to make decisions that no one else is making. Isn't that one of the reasons we dream – to create our own reality?

Exercises

1. Who did you receive your Critical Parent messages from?
2. Who did you receive your Nurturing Parent messages from?
3. Which messages do you need to hear more and which messages do you need to hear less to balance your Parent ego state and live more freely in the present moment?

Reference

Berne, E. (1961). *Transactional Analysis in Psychotherapy: A Systematic Individual and Social Psychiatry*. New York: Grove Press.

10

Dreams and *A Nightmare on Elm Street*

Theory: Dreams

Dreaming is a process that occurs in the mind during the hours of sleep and on recall involves images, narratives and sequences that can appear to be unreal or fantastical.

Movie: *A Nightmare on Elm Street (1984)*

In the fictional town of Springwood, Ohio, teenagers Tina, Rod, Glen and Nancy are being tormented in their dreams by a disfigured predator. One by one, the teenagers come to an untimely death. Director Wes Craven had been inspired by articles printed during the late 70s and early 80s about Southeast Asian refugees dying unexplained deaths during sleep, characterised with nightmare presentations. The article drew Craven's attention to the connective tissue between a terrifying phenomenon occurring in specific cultural communities where people were scared to go to sleep in case they did not wake up and an unconscious part of our psyche where we store what is too terrifying to be consciously known. The movie was an immediate commercial success and Craven's refusal to make the content more family friendly clearly tapped into the cinematic unconscious, people's relationships to dreaming and dreams, and, predominantly, nightmares (Young 2022).

What We're Doing

In this chapter, we will be looking at the act of dreaming and the role it plays viewed through the lens of psychotherapy. Through exploring the characters in *A Nightmare on Elm Street* and their own experience of dreaming, we will learn more about dreams and our connection to them and how we can use our ability to dream to understand ourselves better and live the life we want. Using my own experience in training, I invite you to consider how the theory may relate to your life.

The Greek physician Hippocrates (ca 460–380 BCE) is referred to as the Father of Modern Medicine and it is from him that we have derived the Hippocratic Oath, the ethical criteria that medical professionals observe in patient treatment today. He was one of the earliest champions of the powers of dreams and dream analysis and saw them as a way to heal the body. We have come to associate dreams with psychiatrist Sigmund Freud, whose findings were collated in his 1913 seminal book, *The Interpretation of Dreams*. This was the first time anyone had made real a connection between conscious desire and our state of dreaming.

> *We are alone in taking something else into account. We have introduced a new class of phychical material between the manifest content of dreams and the conclusions of our enquiry [. . .] It is from these dream-thoughts and not from a dreams manifest content that we disentangle this meaning.*
> (Freud 1976, p. 381)

What is Freud saying here? What is the unconscious? How are we to know a place that is unknown? We use the word '*conscious*' as a state of knowing, so, by definition, what is unconscious is a state of unknowing. If we understand the purpose and relevance of psychotherapy as being to help us solve our emotional difficulties, it makes sense to better know the entirety of our situation, understanding the emotional consciousness as well as what is hidden in the emotional depths. But surely this is made slightly problematic when the information we need access to is stored within the vault of our unconscious – an unknown terrain and the only thing known for sure about this terrain is that it cannot be reached. Through their work, Freud and later Carl Jung, a psychiatrist and psychologist, became convinced that the space between the two states was where the gold was buried (Jung 1964a,b). Jung and Freud agreed on the importance of delving into dreams to introduce ourselves to parts of ourselves that have been cut off and feel unreachable but can be discovered when we brave the exploration of our unconscious. Jung felt that careful analysis and exploration of our dreams, of our unconscious, creates a bridge for the psyche; once we are able to make conscious some of what is unconscious, we create more balance in the psyche. They believed that it was in making new connections using an amalgamation of conscious information, recognition and unconscious memories and thoughts, that a person is able to alleviate their emotional struggles and find peace.

This liminal waiting room, if you like, this third, middle dimension, is explored in the therapy room. This is where the therapist uses dreams created and brought by the client, to probe and explore what is being rejected and banished from the conscious realm. It is hypothesised that once what is unknown can be brought into the client's awareness, a new perspective is on offer, one that has the creative potential to shed new light on a troubling situation and release the client from the feeling of being trapped with no choices. This space where we dream is unlimited by structure, reality, form and time. It is boundless and in its very landscape and environment, we find ourselves with a new sense of freedom. This limitlessness illustrates the liberation we are searching for as we strive to free ourselves from the psychological shackles of our existence.

A Nightmare on Elm Street opens with Tina in a central headshot against a blank, white canvas, dreaming. She finds herself running alone in her nightgown through an abandoned boiler room, frightened. A nightmare often holds the dreamer terrified and running for their life in a deserted space. We now know more about the many tunnels the dreamer runs through in sleep, as studies have revealed the importance of the many interconnected components within the area known as the brain's default mode network (DMN), specifically the hippocampus, and how these have been observed to be active during periods of rest while we dream (Desailles et al. 2011).

Changing training institutes was a commitment, for sure. Instead of the one hour door-to-door journey I had been doing in the first year, I was now travelling two hours outside London and needing to stay overnight. But this was not the biggest hurdle. Over coffee, I tell my friend I am moving schools. He happens to know the area and wants to show me this really cool feature next to the train station to which I will travel once a month. He finds a photo on the internet. My gasp is loud and shocks us both. A tightly balled knot of fear dropped in my gut and I was dumbfounded by the strength of my reaction. Two humungous cooling towers dominated the picture. Cooling towers were not something I ever thought about or even noticed as I went about the world, but as I looked at them now, there was no mistaking the feeling in my body. Fear. It made no sense. Yes, I had a recurring dream of cooling towers as a child – a huge, looming, colossal tower threatening in its sheer size and then a feeling of powerlessness and paralysing fear that I am trapped inside – but so what? A nightmare where I was all alone, no one could see me, no one knew I was there, no one would find me. Inside the tower, I did not move. I sat terrified, crouched, still, the kind of paralysis only experienced in the dreamstate, the release from which is often found by waking, screaming or finally descending into a non-dream-filled slumber. A friend showing me a photo of my childhood nightmare years later, a silly nightmare and one which I had not had for decades, triggered that same paralysis.

One does not become enlightened by imagining figures of light, but by making the darkness conscious. (Jung 1945, CW13, p. 335)

'*All day long I've been seeing that guy's weird face,*' Tina tells her friend Nancy about a guy in her dream. To the girls' surprise, Nancy reveals she has also experienced the same dream. Later they find out that their friend Rod has had the exact same one too and, as they voice their dreams, it becomes clear it is actually more of a collective nightmare.

In the Jungian therapy room, dreams elicit behavioural change. We begin to walk the earth with a different consciousness. Jungian analysis focuses on dreams as a part of the therapy in a more alchemical way than typical Freudian analysis, something akin to the spinning of straw into gold as remembered in the fairy tale *Rumpelstiltskin*. Fairy tales are viewed as the oldest body of collective works in humanity, illustrating archetypal and eternal psychological expressions. Jung's belief is not only in a personal unconscious which can find its way into our dreams but in a collective unconscious (Jung CW 9.1, 1967). This societal unconscious not only refers to a personality of the age we are living in but also spans ancestral time and space, holding within it that which society itself finds hard to tolerate. It constitutes that which is banished because society does not want/cannot bear to look at it. But what is rejected finds its way back into our psyche through our dreams. In *A Nightmare on Elm Street*, the predator is a child murderer named Freddy Kruger who has found his way into the brains of teenagers as retribution for the parents who burned him alive years earlier. Trauma is passed on through the generations. Craven's movie taps into the power of the unconscious, both personally and collectively.

As Nancy sleeps, we see Kruger try his best to rip through a pierceable fabric with his fingers - made deadly by the homemade metal knives he has fashioned and attached to them. The fabric is thin yet somehow durable, creating for Nancy a physical separation between her dream world and her real one. In this scene, Craven uses the flimsy partition between worlds to illustrate the ease and inevitability with which the brain switches into a different operating system. While we sleep, we encounter worlds of anomalies in scaling – an oversized Freddy Kruger in the doorway. We experience contextual disassociation – writhing maggots comprising the flesh beneath Kruger's skin. Distortions of this nature during dreams can be seen as neurologically consistent with increased activity in the occipital-temporal visual regions of the brain and heightened activity in the amygdala. The amygdala is the smoke alarm for our brain, warning us of danger. However, if we are left without adequate support from other areas of the waking cognitive recognition process, the amygdala cannot efficiently deduce what is real and what is imagined, including in our sleep, and especially in our nightmares (Desailles et al. 2011).

'In each of us there is another whom we do not know. He speaks to us in dreams and tells us how differently he sees us from the way we see ourselves. When, therefore, we find ourselves in a difficult situation to which there is no solution, he can sometimes kindle a light that radically alters our attitude – the very attitude that led us into the difficult situation.' (Jung 1964a,b, CW 10 para. 325)

I started drawing. Remembering Spielberg's movie *Close Encounters of the Third Kind* and Roy Neary's drawings of the huge cooling tower-esque image he kept seeing in his mind, I started to draw larger and larger pictures of these cooling towers attempting to get a little closer to the fear, an attempt to be on the bridge between my conscious and unconscious even if I was scared to walk across it. And come September walk across is what I did, or, more accurately, took the train. The number of times I used the toilet on the journey! When you are scared, even your pee wants to run away! When I finally got to the station, I sat on the bench for a long while just staring at these huge structures which had held something frightening for my Child inside them all these years. I cried and realised that you don't always have to know why you are crying but simply acknowledge there is a sadness, a need to grieve a loss.

I had imagined that the first night I spent in my new school, there might be a special place designated for laying down my sleeping bag but, when I got there, I was told I could bed down anywhere in the whole building. Surely the office was out of bounds but this was not specified. I loved the idea of sleeping in the library – I didn't have a revolver but I liked to think of myself as Miss Scarlett. I pushed the table and chairs to the side of the little room walled with books. It felt very grown up in this small space, freeing, as if I could go anywhere I wanted and that would be where I belonged. As if every choice I made was my own. That night I did not dream I went to Manderlay (Chapter 9) but instead dreamt of the cooling towers and that night, for the first time ever, the dream felt different. I was inside the tower but I was not powerless. The emphasis had shifted from paralysis to a more active fear. I could sense I was not alone, that my fear now involved another entity, something I hoped I could outrun. Never before had I ever dreamt of anything, or anyone, inside the cooling towers other than me.

My new tutor, Pagan, has a dreamlike quality all of her own. She has long grey hair pinned with a pencil in a loose bun. Wisdom and age sparkle underneath watery blue, glittery eyelids. In her long flowing dress, she floats across the carpet, inviting us to find a dream that we would like to discuss with our partner. Considering this suggestion, I become aware of profound feelings of shame and loss which are hiding within me, inside the cooling tower of my unconscious. I look around the room to find a partner that makes me feel safe, someone non-threatening, maybe even an ally. Dreams try to speak to us and Jung encourages us to turn towards the dream and introduce ourselves. A metaphorical shaking of hands with this new and unknown part of us. Pagan is Balinese and talks about how different cultures have been using dreams since humans have been alive, in an effort to make sense of the world around them. She talks about what would happen if we truly contemplated the vast expanse of life, the sheer unpredictability and randomness of it all, our absolute powerlessness when faced with the enormity of living, and how easily we can become overwhelmed. Dreams are a happening with something bigger than ourselves. Are we ready to accept such an invitation from the unconscious?

GLEN: *You ever read about the Balinese way of dreaming?*
NANCY: *No.*
GLEN: *They got a whole system they call 'dream skills'. So, if you have a nightmare, for instance like falling, right?*
NANCY: *Yeah.*
GLEN: *Instead of screaming and going nuts, you say, ok, I'm gonna make up my mind that I fall into a magic world where I can get something special, like a poem or song. They get all their art literature from dreams. Just wake up and write it down. Dream skills.*
NANCY: *And what if they meet a monster in their dream? Then what?*
GLEN: *They turn their back on it. Takes away its energy, and it disappears.*

After paying attention to her personal dreams, turning herself to the dream and introducing herself, as well as paying close attention to the dreams of her friends, Nancy has a dream where she brings Kruger's hat back from her dream life into her waking life. She devises a plan to catch Kruger in her dream and bring him into her reality where she asks her policeman father to be ready to arrest him. Nancy affects a behavioural change which saves her life.

Making the decision to change my training institute felt like a massive and liberating decision, bringing me closer to mammoth-sized cooling towers, structures which had dominated my dream life in childhood. As I explore my dreams in therapy, the figure I run from does not chase me back. I feel it is a spirit I have known my whole life. The presence cannot come to me but demands I go to them. It can come, it is able to, but does not. I run, but I am running in circles. The spirit is a woman, and I cannot escape her. I am frightened to go to her yet at the same time desperate to go to her. I don't know how to get near her. As I look around the tower, I see nothing but my feelings: shame, loss, guilt and love. I play with the feelings, turning them into separate strands and then twisting the strands to form a rope. The rope ties itself around my waist and I feel the spirit of the cooling tower pulling me towards her. There is nothing in the darkness but an instinctive submission of my body, allowing the rope I have created from my feelings to pull me closer to a powerful and terrifying force I cannot see. When I reach her, she is without a face, without a form, but I would know that feeling anywhere. The feeling of yearning. Of needing. Of hoping. Of fearing. The child as it looks up to see itself in her eyes. It is my mother.

Exercises

1. Choose a dream. What feelings were you experiencing in your dream? Are these feelings you are comfortable with in your daily life? Do they remind you of a situation in your life?
2. If you were to give the dream a different ending, what would it be? What does this ending mean to you?
3. Imagine the dream again but with you as a different character in the dream. How do you feel about the dream in the body of someone or even something else? It doesn't have to be a person, e.g. what am I feeling as the cooling tower, what am I feeling as the rope?

References

Desailles, M., Dang-Vu, T.T., Sterpenich, V. et al. (2011). Cognitive and emotional processes during dreaming: a neuroimaging view. http://www.mentalhealth sciences.com/docs/Consciousness2011.pdf (accessed 5 February 2025).

Freud, S. (1976). *The Pelican Freud Library, Vol. 4: The Interpretation of Dreams,* 1976. London: Penguin Books.

Jung, C.G. (1945). The philosophical tree. In: *Alchemical Studies* (The Collected Works of C.G. Jung, Vol. 13: Civilization in Transition, trans. R. F. C. Hull) (ed. H. Read, M. Fordham, and G. Adler). London: Routledge & Kegan Paul.

Jung, C.G. (1964a). *Dreams* (trans. R.F.C. Hull). Princeton, NJ: Princeton University Press.

Jung, C.G. (1964b). The meaning of psychology for modern man. In: *Civilisation in Transition* (Collected Works of C.G. Jung, Vol. 10: Civilization in Transition, trans. R.F.C. Hull) (ed. H. Read, M. Fordham, and G. Adler). London: Routledge & Kegan Paul.

Jung, C.G. (1967). *The Archetypes and The Collective Unconscious* (The Collected Works of C.G. Jung, Vol 9, Part 1). Princeton, NJ: Princeton University Press.

Young, H. (2022). Craven, Wes. http://www.sensesofcinema.com/2022/great-directors/craven-wes (accessed 5 February 2025).

11

Co-dependence/Symbiosis and *CODA*

Theory: Co-dependence/Symbiosis

Symbiosis is defined as both a development phase characterised by a lack of differentiation between self and others and a relationship which is contingent upon the family and social network. (Richman 1978, p. 139)

Co-dependence is a defensive strategy of attachment where two or more people form a psychological enmeshment where they rely on aspects of each other for emotional survival.

Movie: *CODA (2021)*

Ruby Rossi, 17 years old, is the youngest child and only member of her family who can hear. Her mother Jackie, her father Frank and brother Leo are all deaf. Ruby uses sign language to communicate with them and also translate for them – and she always has. She gets up before school to help in the family's fishing business and the plan is for her to become more involved in the company when she finishes school. When Ruby sees her crush, Miles, sign up for choir she is suddenly emboldened to do the same. The choir teacher, Bernardo, is intrigued but also confused as to why Ruby is scared to sing in public. She tells him that children used to make fun of her because she spoke like a deaf person. Bernardo thinks she has a voice '*worth hearing*' and elects to tutor her privately to enable her to apply for a scholarship place at a music school. As Ruby's passion for music develops and her confidence grows, there are fewer hours in the day to help her family. For the first time, the Rossi family are forced to see the extent to which they have depended on Ruby. This brings up inner conflict for everyone as they must confront their fear of change and of loss.

What We're Doing

In this chapter, we will be looking at the psychological theory of co-dependence/symbiosis through the eyes of the movie's main character, Ruby, in the film *CODA*. As we learn about the theory, we will use it to understand and explore Ruby's enmeshed relationship with her family. Using my own experience in training, I invite you to consider how the theory may relate to your life.

Arriving at school a little late, I was surprised to see that my usual seat was taken. I always sat next to Abigail, third seat from the door on the light-pink sofa just underneath the window, but today someone else was sitting there. In that moment, I noticed I had become dependent on the space next to Abigail being mine. I move across the room to a new seat to find out that Pagan has asked half the class to sit in completely different seats. Aha! So, the change had been engineered. But why? Why tamper with a perfectly working model? The handout read, 'Symbiosis.' Reading about the theory of symbiosis, something takes me to co-dependence, a term I remember from the Alcoholics Anonymous (AA) literature I had read whilst trying to understand more about my father's addiction. In AA, the word is used to describe a relationship between a person and a chemical substance that they had come to depend on and also the role of the family in trying to support the individual to wean themselves off the substance and come to health. The family became the co-dependents. However, the idea of co-dependence had existed for years in psychotherapeutic theory and over time, the term evolved into the description of a particular style of attachment between people.

In *CODA*, Frank, Jackie and Leo are all dependent upon Ruby, who has herself known nothing else but this particular dynamic. Her world, for as long as she can remember, has been about using her ability to hear to help her family who cannot. When Ruby begins showing signs of pulling away from the family business and developing her passion for singing, her mother Jackie doesn't understand why Ruby would want to do that.

JACKIE:　[signing] *If I was blind would you want to be a painter?*
RUBY:　[signing and speaking] *Why is it always about you?*

Jackie has grown so dependent on Ruby that she dismisses Ruby's desire to sing because it does not serve her own interests. Ruby and Jackie's co-dependent style of attachment means that if one of them threatens to leave the enmeshment, then the others' survival is threatened, too.

I wondered about my attachment to the seat next to Abigail and realised it wasn't the light-pink sofa that I was attached to but Abigail herself. In a new school, a class full of strangers doing intense and deeply emotional excavations, I had sought out someone who reminded me of a sister. Someone familiar, someone I trusted, someone who I imagined would understand me. Sitting next to Abigail had been keeping me emotionally safe.

RUBY: [signing] *Did you ever wish I was deaf?*
JACKIE: [signing] *When you were born, at the hospital, they gave you a hearing test. And there you were, so tiny and sweet, with those electrodes all over you. And I. . . prayed that you would be deaf. When they told us that you were hearing, I felt. . . My heart sank.*
RUBY: [signing] *Why?*
JACKIE: [signing] *I was worried that we wouldn't connect. Like me and my mom, we're not close. I thought I would fail you. That being deaf would make me a bad mom.*

Jackie fears the loss of connection with her daughter as soon as Ruby is born. To prevent the pain of such a loss, she would rather her daughter come into the world without one of her five senses than Jackie bear the 'badness' of failing her as a mother. Jackie fears the legacy of maternal distance, remembering the distance between her and her own mother. She thinks Ruby being born deaf and mother and daughter being co-dependent is a better scenario than Ruby being born with hearing and independent.

For Jackie, she cannot bear the shame of failing at motherhood as well as feeling the loss of a close connection with her daughter. She relies on their emotional co-dependence to avoid facing feelings of shame and loss. She fosters and encourages a symbiotic connection and transfers her shame to Ruby if Ruby should question the relationship and want to live her life in a way that might not include Jackie. When Ruby attempts to do the things she wants to do in her own life – like singing – she is forced to cope with a pervading sense of guilt, which dominates and serves to maintain her loss of autonomy.

The diagram below (Fig. 11.1) is an ideal situation. It shows healthy symbiosis (Schiff et al. 1975). Jackie is the primary parent and all her three ego states (Chapters 1, 2 and 9) are shown to be fully functioning (unbroken line) taking care of the Child ego state of newborn baby Ruby. Ruby's Parent and Adult ego states are shown with broken lines to denote Ruby having no access to these parts yet, as they have not yet formed. The outer line, which wraps around all Jackie's ego states and Ruby's Child ego state, denotes the normal position for a new mother and how we expect a parent/caregiver to behave in caring for a newborn baby.

Slowly, and as baby Ruby grows, she will develop autonomy and independence and her Parent and Adult ego states will develop. As a young child, Ruby quickly learned that being able to hear was something that could keep her separate from her family. She also learned that by focussing on her

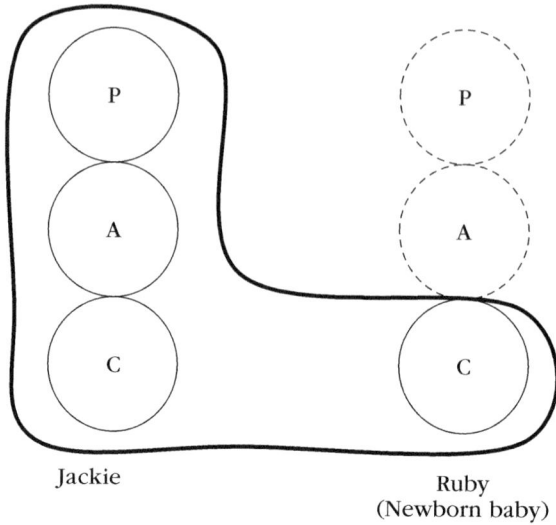

Fig. 11.1 Healthy symbiosis between Jackie and newborn baby Ruby

maturation processes - e.g. over-functioning and fast development of her
Parent and Adult ego states - to the exclusion of more developmental immature stages of her child development, she was able to be the bridge between
her family and the rest of the world. In being a translator for them all and
serving all of their needs before her own, she opened up more possibilities for
them. Though this ensured Ruby's emotional survival in the short term,
there was a cost to Ruby long term of closing down possibilities for herself.
Ruby's over-developed Adult ego state and her Parentification (Chapter 8), an
over-developed Parent ego state, compromised the development of her own
Child ego state.

RUBY [SIGNING]:   *How is music rude but Tinder's okay?*
JACKIE [SIGNING]: *Because Tinder is something we can all do as a family.*

Ruby is scrolling on her phone, wanting to listen to her music. Jackie
does not want phones at the table, but when Leo wants to look at his
phone for Tinder, it feels different for Jackie. This is something where the
whole family can be included, unlike Ruby's music, which no one can hear
other than Ruby.

In Ruby's enmeshment, the survival threat involved is not only a threat
to her own psychological safety but the safety of her mother, father and
brother too. How will they hear without her? What will happen to them in
the world if they cannot hear? What will happen to them and to her if they
are laughed at? Ruby tells her friend Miles that he has no idea how it feels
to have people laugh at your family and also be the only one who could

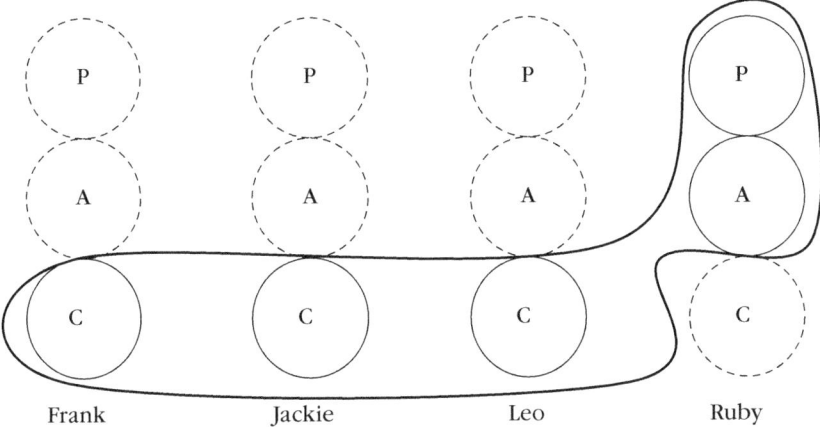

Fig. 11.2   Symbiosis between Ruby and her Family

hear it, as often her family would not know other people were mocking them. This is a form of vicarious trauma – the psychological pain and impact of watching another person suffer whilst being helpless to intervene. As a young child, Ruby found that the best way to alleviate the pain she experienced witnessing the world laugh at the people she loved was by helping them as much as she possibly could. In helping them, she also helped herself to feel better; less angry, less sad, less scared.

In Fig. 11.2, we can see the Parent, Adult and Child ego states of the whole family. Remembering the broken lines as indicative of ego states not completely formed yet (refer to Fig. 11.1), we can see how Ruby uses her overdeveloped Parent and Adult ego states to look after the Child ego states of each of her family members, whilst abandoning her own Child ego state.

The typical process of individuation, where a person outgrows their environment and physically, emotionally and psychologically separates from the parent/caregiver, was not available to Ruby, as for Ruby the protection of her family was more important. Ruby's friend Gertie highlights the family's co-dependent relationships when she says of Leo, '*I'm sure he doesn't need his little sister protecting him.*' Whilst Ruby and her family are protecting change to the status quo, the family's growth is inhibited, as a person's growth, biologically and psychologically, is born from change. Though the film is about people with disabilities, it perhaps uncharacteristically does not follow the typical trajectory of fostering audience empathy for the characters who are deaf but instead portrays Ruby as suffering a disability of her own, that of co-dependence.

CODA encourages the audience to consider emotional and physical disabilities in a different way and see co-dependence in the same way as they view society's stereotypical definitions of what constitutes dysfunction.

Leo is the first of the family who wants to grow his Parent and Adult ego states and move out of symbiosis. Ruby behaves as Leo's symbiotic Parent ego state, whilst Leo wants to assert and develop his under-developed Adult ego state. '*I'm a grown man,*' he answers when asked if he would like his sister to be called in to help. His desire for change and to form his own opinions and move away from the one-family-brain-mindset shows Leo's resistance to the symbiosis. '*I was handling it, you made me look stupid,*' says Leo to Ruby, annoyed when Ruby intervenes in a business conversation he would have liked to have had himself. Ruby steps in to avoid Leo being taken advantage of, but in rescuing him (Chapter 6), she also strips Leo of the ability to learn for himself how to advocate for himself.

Features of unhealthy symbiosis or co-dependence in Adults:

- The absorption or rejection involving one or more of another's ego states.
- A psychological threat to one person affects the psychological survival of the other.
- Protection of the co-dependent organism takes precedence.
- Options for growth are inhibited as the perspective is fear-driven and limited only to the growth of one organism rather than two.

Examples of how these features manifest as symptoms:

1. **Discounting**. The unconscious practice of minimising a feeling in the self, an aspect of a problem, or other people in order to make less important what is actually significant.
   Discounting of the self – Ruby might say, '*there is nothing I can do.*'
   Discounting the significance of the problem – Ruby might say, '*it's not a big deal if I don't sing in the choir.*'
   Discounting the ability to solve the problem – Ruby might say, '*there's no one else to help my family but me.*'
   Discounting the problem – Ruby might say, '*singing isn't important to me.*'
2. **Grandiosity** – This includes an intentional exaggeration that justifies the person's behaviour.
   Ruby might say, '*there is no one else that knows how to help my family like I can because I am the one who has done it all my life.*'
3. **Agitation** – Internal stress which comes out as restlessness, nervousness, anxiety or irritability.
   Ruby might become irritated with her family and others as she battles the internal conflict within herself relating to what she wants versus how it makes her feel to choose what her family might not want.
   Ruby might scream, '*I just don't know what to do!*'
4. **Violence** – Ruby might break something or try to hurt someone, or herself, as a desperate display of repressed emotion contained

within her body. These emotions are anger towards herself and her family, sadness towards herself and her family, fear for herself in separating from her family and fear for her family in being in the world without her.

When the family are lined up to have a big interview on their new solo venture, a fishing business, it clashes with Ruby's music schedule.

JACKIE [SIGNING]:	*This is important.*
RUBY [SIGNING AND SPEAKING]:	*My stuff is important too!*
JACKIE [SIGNING]:	*Do it!*
RUBY [SIGNING AND SPEAKING]:	*I can't!*
JACKIE [SIGNING]:	*You want us to fail?*

Jackie's fear of being in the world without Ruby is palpable, but instead of expressing her fear with honesty, she projects it onto Ruby in the form of co-dependent scapegoating. Ruby now carries a feeling of guilt, she misses her singing tutorial with her teacher and stays to help her family with the interview, an added layer of suppressed sadness. Later, when her teacher lambasts her for wasting an opportunity to attend a music school, Ruby confesses, '*I've never done anything without my family before.*' Ruby's Child ego state is scared. She does not know what it is like to be in the world on her own, as she has been locked in a symbiotic relationship with her family since she was born.

Frank and Jackie discuss the possibility of Ruby going to music school and Jackie reveals she is worried in case Ruby fails. She is also concerned about what the remaining family, herself included, will do without Ruby. When Jackie refers to her as '*her baby,*' Frank clarifies, '*she was never a baby.*' Jackie's comment to Frank illustrates the blind spot aspect of co-dependence that exists between a parent and a child. Frank's comment to Jackie illustrates the expected biological and emotional developmental stages of growth; that the child will separate from the parent, and the fact that this is not something Ruby has been able to do.

RUBY [SIGNING]:	*You need a hearing deckhand.*
FRANK [SIGNING]:	*Yeah, that's you! You were that person!*
RUBY [SIGNING AND SPEAKING]:	*I can't always be that person!*

When Ruby decides she must prioritise the family business over school and music, Leo is irritated. He refers to her as Saint Ruby. Though this comment is intended as a passive-aggressive insult, there is more than a grain of truth in the martyrdom Ruby exhibits and that co-dependence and symbiosis can foster. Jackie is unwilling to admit the emotional damage being done to Ruby and explains Leo's irritability as '*complicated,*' saying that '*he feels left out.*' Jackie is referring to Leo feeling this way from a co-dependence point of view, however, Leo is trying to break the co-dependence and end the symbiosis, and until the rest of the family do the same, Leo may indeed feel left out. What Jackie omits in her explanation to Ruby is her own part in Leo feeling left out.

LEO [SIGNING]:   *They'll keep looking to you for everything.*
RUBY [SIGNING]:   *What else am I supposed to do?*
LEO [SIGNING]:   *Let me do this! I got this! I'm the older brother. And I get treated like a baby.*

CODA's director chooses to shoot Ruby's solo at the music concert without audio, so that the audience watching the movie can hear what Ruby's parents hear – which is silence. That evening, Frank and Ruby are alone and Frank asks Ruby to sign the song so he can actually understand what his daughter was saying. Frank was already troubled about Ruby's decision to quit school, and then he heard the lyrics of 'All I Need to Get By' (composed by Ashford & Simpson), and he knew that it was time to be the parent and look after his child by letting her go and helping her to let go:

> *I'll sacrifice for you*
> *Dedicate my life to you*
> *I will go where you lead*
> *Always there in time of need.*

The next morning, Frank, Jackie and Leo cancel fishing and surprise Ruby by taking her to her music audition instead. Ruby is accepted at music school and decides to go. When the time comes to leave, she hugs her family and drives away, but quickly stops the car and runs back to her family for a second hug. The second hug acknowledges the fear they have all surmounted, the love they share and the growth they all need.

At the end of the weekend, Pagan informed the class that where we were sitting would be our designated seats for next term. I started to consider the co-dependent and symbiotic relationships in my own family and the impact of that on all of us and how it impacted our attachment to others and how we showed up in the world. Co-dependence is a difficult condition to identify as it can first present under the guise of the 'happy' or 'close' family. The reality is much more serious as it reduces development in the entire organism, including cognitive and behavioural processing, the development of emotional intelligence and subsequent volitional agency and moral judgement (Raklova 2013).

Exercises

1. Is there someone in your life you easily go to rescue or who easily comes to rescue you? Is there someone you believe cannot do certain things for themselves and so you believe it is your responsibility to do for them? Or someone who takes responsibility for certain things in your life that you believe you cannot do for yourself?
2. Are there things in your life you might be sacrificing for another or someone else who might be sacrificing things they want in life to give something to you?
3. Are there relationships in your life where you behave in a certain way because you worry about what might happen otherwise?

References

Raklova, E. (2013). Symbiosis problems in codependent families. https://www.hrpub.org/download/20131201/UJP2-19400948.pdf (accessed 19 August 2025).

Richman, J. (1978). Symbiosis, empathy, suicidal behaviour and the family. https://onlinelibrary.wiley.com/doi/epdf/10.1111/j.1943-278X.1978.tb00581.x (accessed 19 August 2025).

Schiff, A., Mellor, K., Schiff, E. et al. (1975). *Cathexis Reader: Transactional Analysis Treatment of Psychosis*. New York: Harper Row.

12

Attachment Theory and *Frozen*

Theory: Attachment Theory

Attachment theory is a psychological theory where the attachment between babies and their primary caregivers/mothers sets the foundation for the style of attachment an individual will go on to develop in adulthood. There are four attachment styles: secure, anxious, avoidant and disorganised (Bowlby 1969).

Movie: *Frozen (2013)*

Inspired by the Hans Christian Andersen fairy tale, *The Snow Queen*, the film *Frozen* is a story of two sisters, Elsa and Anna. Elsa has the magical powers of cryokinesis, the psychic ability to create ice and snow. Being young and still unaware of how to use her powers, she accidentally injures her sister Anna. Her frightened parents, the King and Queen of Arendelle, take Anna to the trolls who erase her memory of Elsa's powers as well as the accident. They recommend locking Elsa up in a tower so she cannot cause any more harm. The girls grow up in isolation, physically and emotionally distanced from each other as well as other people. Years later, the girl's parents drown at sea. Elsa is crowned Queen and the public is allowed into the castle for the first time where Prince Hans, a suitor from a neighbouring kingdom, proposes to Anna. Elsa is unhappy with the union and her anger reveals her powers in front of the people of Arendelle for the first time. The people are frightened and Elsa is accused of witchcraft. She escapes to North Mountain where she builds herself an ice palace, oblivious to the fact that back in Arendelle, her outburst of power has plummeted the town into a deadly winter freeze. Anna, with the help of a few friends, begins the treacherous trek to save her sister and her home.

What We're Doing

In this chapter, we will be looking at attachment theory in the movie *Frozen*. As we learn about the four different styles of attachment, we will use them to understand the attachment styles of Elsa and Anna, the movie's two main characters. Using my own experience in training, I invite you to consider how the theory may relate to your life.

The Oxford dictionary defines '*attach*' as '*to join or fasten something to something else.*' Interestingly, the example sentence is to '*attach your safety line to the bridge.*' It's as if without even trying, or despite not trying, the editors chose to talk about safety. Why is this interesting? Because safety is intrinsically connected to our survival and therefore our attachment to others is directly related to our need to survive. Humans need connection. How we choose to do that is different for everyone.

Mary Ainsworth and John Bowlby published research that formed the foundation of attachment theory as it is known today. In the 'Strange Situation Test,' Ainsworth studied children's reactions when they were left alone in a room and their parent departed (Ainsworth and Bell 1970). She discovered three distinct groups of responses. The first group, defined as secure attachment, was upset at the parent leaving but then happy to be comforted when the parent reappeared. The second group, defined as anxious attachment, was heavily distressed at the parent leaving and, despite wanting comfort when the parent reappeared, would push against being soothed. The third group, defined as avoidant attachment, showed minor or no obvious distress when the parent left and when the parent reappeared the child would act similarly unfazed and not look to establish contact. However, measuring the heart rates and stress hormone levels of the third group's participants confirmed that the child's experience of their parent departing did, in fact, include internal distress which they were externally concealing, showing our ability to mask at such a young age. The fourth attachment style is disorganised attachment, featuring aspects of both the avoidant attachment style and also the anxious attachment style, with the main feature being an incoherence and unpredictability in pattern and behaviour (Main and Solomon 1990).

Thinking about my psychotherapy training, it often felt like I was part of a strange situation. Eighteen people who did not know each other, regularly meeting and speaking about our innermost thoughts, conducting excavations into calcified memories to reveal the darkest, most painful moments in our childhoods. If it was a test, it felt like the result wasn't a pass or fail but rather information about yourself to help understand why, when trying to form attachments with others, it might sometimes feel as if you were passing or failing. There were people I found it so easy to attach to, loving the qualities of their personalities, and then there were others from whom I physically distanced myself, feeling unable to connect. Learning about attachment theory not only shed light on these current relationships but helped me start to learn about the relationships in my family, the first group of humans I'd ever known and where I had first tried to attach and learnt about attachment.

At the beginning of *Frozen*, we meet the sisters when they are very young and Anna is trying to coax Elsa out of a peaceful slumber. Suddenly, Anna has an epiphany and knows the best way to wake up Elsa. '*Do you want to build a snowman?*' Anna asks. This appears to be sister code (as well as a great song) as the next moment Elsa is running down the stairs holding her sister's hand excitedly, Anna goading her, '*Do the magic!*' Elsa makes a snowball and then a snowfall and then turns the floor into an ice rink, Anna exclaiming, '*This is amazing!*' Elsa continues using her ice- and snow-making gift to delight her sister and creates a snowman whom she names Olaf. She hides behind him and puts on a funny voice to try to bring him to life. Anna throws her arms around Olaf and says, '*I love you, Olaf.*'

Elsa manifests snow mountain after snow mountain and Anna jumps from one to the other becoming giddy with excitement. Elsa warns her to '*slow down*' but Anna is having so much fun that she jumps faster, too fast for Elsa to make the next mountain in time. Elsa slips and Anna appears about to fall. Elsa tries to save Anna but in doing so her power accidentally strikes Anna who drops to the ground, motionless. Elsa holds her sister lovingly, '*It's ok, Anna, I got you.*' When her parents arrive they exclaim, '*Elsa, what have you done? This is getting out of hand.*'

Her parents take Anna to the trolls for help. The head troll advises removal of all magic and memories of magic, '*She won't remember I have powers?*' Elsa asks. Elsa's parents lock the palace gates and keep Elsa away from Anna. They are sure that '*limiting her contact with people,*' and keeping her powers '*hidden from everyone*' is the '*solution until she learns control.*' Elsa's father teaches her the mantra, '*Conceal, don't feel, don't let it show.*'

In wishing to keep their children safe, Elsa's parents believed that their decisions were the best for Elsa. Elsa believed them because that is what little children do – they place trust in those they form attachments with and defer to those in power. Elsa has formed attachments with Anna and her parents and these attachments with her family – her first experience of a group – are made to keep Elsa safe and secure in the world. Protecting these attachments becomes imperative to Elsa and the story that evolves to help her do so becomes as important in how Elsa goes on to live her life and the decisions she makes. It is the earliest interactions in Elsa's life, the ones from the past, that go on to shape her experiences in the present and future. Forcing the girls apart, from each other and from everybody else, had a direct impact on how they formed attachments, how they viewed themselves and how they showed up in the world.

Elsa – avoidant attachment:

- Elsa is the emotional heart of the story and yet suppresses all her emotions. The opening scene is of thick ice which must be cut through with an ice saw to reach the water. The song that accompanies the scene is *'Beware the Frozen Heart,'* a metaphor for Elsa's emotions becoming deeply buried. The ice in the movie is a pathetic fallacy, the coldness, remoteness and frozen state of Elsa's emotional internal world.
- Elsa is reluctant to get close to other people, *'don't let them in'* is what she believes she must do. She has a fear of social intimacy, *'don't let them know,'* and keeps her relationships few and distant.
- Elsa buys into a story created by her parents to help her explain the struggle she faces in the world. *'I am dangerous.' 'I can hurt others.' 'There is something wrong with me.'*
- Elsa is unable to access her emotions, which would allow her to process her grief from traumatic events that happen in her life – her parents' death and her estrangement from Anna.
- Elsa, by rejecting herself, also rejects Anna.
- Elsa feels she has no choice. She must be the *'good girl'* and *'put on a show.'*
- Elsa sets rigid boundaries that are intended to keep everyone out.

Elsa was left alone to cope with the sadness, fear and guilt of hurting Anna. Her father's instruction not to feel encouraged Elsa to deactivate her body's biological emotional sensors. The non-verbal message was that Elsa's feelings were bad. By denying her basic feelings, Elsa now starts to overvalue her self-reliance and avoid the acknowledgement of any weakness or vulnerability. Elsa has had no opportunity to process the sadness or fear of hurting Anna, cope with the uncertainty of what will happen to Anna or forgive herself for what was an accident. Early formative experiences like these are teeming with learning opportunities, for Elsa to prepare herself for life in adulthood and potentially distressing experiences like coping with sadness and life's uncertainty. What she learns about herself and the world as a young girl will determine how she manages her feelings in response to life's events going forward.

Anna – anxious attachment:

- Anna falls in love with the first man she meets and agrees to marry him. She is desperate to be in a relationship with someone, anyone, and grabs on to the first few things they have in common – like sandwiches – to justify their union.
- Anna is upset and insecure about her relationship with Elsa, not knowing why Elsa shuts her out. She becomes preoccupied/obsessed with the

relationship and is trying her hardest to get Elsa to open up and explain what has happened so she can stop living with this confusion.

- Anna is planning to invite her fiancé Hans' 12 brothers to live at the palace with them. Anna's concerns and preoccupations with family and being with others mean that she confuses her priorities. She delays her own individuation and relationship to herself and does not consider taking the time to get to know her future husband who she has known for a day.

- Anna apologises for things that are not her fault. *'I didn't mean to make you freeze the summer, I'm sorry, it's all my fault.'* Anna would rather assume blame to restore the connection, but this eventually leads to her suppressing anger and resentment.

- Anna expects Elsa to be with her wherever and whenever they are able to be together. Anna romanticises their childhood relationship and finds it hard to accept the way things now are. Having her formative attachment bonds severed without care or repair, Anna finds it hard to be alone and self-soothe.

- Anna finds it hard to be assertive. *'We leave now,'* she tells her friend Kristoff, and then hides behind the door taking a deep breath to calm herself down for having articulated her needs so directly.

- Anna is talkative, emotionally expressive and vulnerable. *'I'm going to talk to my sister.'*

- Anna sets porous boundaries that are intended to let everyone in.

Anna was left alone to cope with the confusion, sadness and loneliness of being forcibly separated from her sister and her own memories. Elsa's instruction, *'Stay away and you'll be safe from me,'* encouraged Anna to deactivate her body's biological emotional sensors. The non-verbal message was that Anna's feelings were wrong. By denying her basic feelings, Anna now starts to become fixated on needing to know and understand what is happening. Anna has had no opportunity to process the rejection she has felt in her body since her estrangement from her sister. She has unprocessed anger, developed as a result of wanting to change a situation she does not understand, and the confusion of not knowing what she has done to make her sister not want to play with her anymore. Early formative experiences like these are teeming with learning opportunities for Anna to prepare herself for life in adulthood. Anna will need to learn how to cope with future distressing experiences, with sadness and life's uncertainty, and what she learns about herself and the world as a young girl will determine how she manages her feelings in response to life's events.

Three years after the sisters' parents died at sea, it is time for Elsa's coronation as Queen. Having had no opportunity to understand herself, who she is and how she inhabits the world, to build resilience and learn tolerance, Elsa loses control of her powers and in exposing herself sees the kingdom of Arendelle turn against her. Elsa flees, beginning the long and lonely walk to North Mountain. Despite her isolation and alienation, we see her using her powers freely and enjoying herself with her gifts for the first time in years. As Elsa sings the iconic song 'Let it Go' she talks about how the 'perfect girl is gone' – Elsa speaks of a freedom to allow the part of herself she has hidden away all these years to be free, gleefully running up the staircase turning everything she can into ice sculptures. After her 'imperfect' behaviour as a child that injured her sister, Elsa was forced into behaving 'perfectly.' Hiding parts of herself limited her potential, making her unhappy. The cost of this subversion is revealed as we see her literally let her hair down. Transformed, Elsa says, 'I never knew what I was capable of.'

Elsa shows how the attachment story can begin to change. When she was keeping part of herself locked away, she was imprisoned not only in the actual castle but internally as well. The self, Elsa's identity, was in conflict with other parts. By loving the part of herself that was banished for all those years, Elsa is learning to build a secure attachment within herself. She is changing her narrative and demonstrating that creating our own internal secure attachment models can modify an earlier-formed, less emotionally regulated, attachment style.

Attaching is something we do our whole lives. It is not a pathological dependency but rather an innately human experience. We all need to connect and attach and if our relationship to ourselves is fragile or fractured, we see this mirrored in our attachments with others. It also changes over the course of our life and is shaped and influenced by ongoing attachments. Olaf is an outward expression of an unconscious secure attachment that Anna and Elsa shared in early childhood.

Secure attachment:

- Regulation of one's own emotional feelings.
- Knowledge of being both loved and lovable.
- Ability to set appropriate boundaries when needed.
- Expression of positive and negative emotions in relationships.
- Equally content being alone or in a relationship.
- Possession of good problem-solving skills and emotional resilience.

Disorganised attachment:

- Anxiety regarding intimacy and social situations creating fear and avoidance.
- Push and pull dynamics in relationships.
- Fear of rejection and abandonment.
- Split off parts of the self for unconscious protection/survival and to prevent rejection and abandonment.
- Trauma response: a mix of freeze, flight and fight with limited understanding of the triggers which reactivate the trauma cycle.

- Difficulty setting appropriate boundaries.
- Mood swings; easily led to emotional dysregulation.

I have formed an attachment in my training group with someone who reminds me of my sister, where I had an early experience of a secure attachment. I also notice that I have moved away from those who remind me of my mother, with whom I had an avoidant attachment. Interestingly, I have found it easiest to form relationships with those who remind me of my father, with whom I formed an anxious attachment. It is imperative to understand that we cannot view attachment styles as good or bad. They can be avenues into a more balanced relationship with the self and others, allowing for a developing understanding of and compassion for younger parts of ourselves that were emotionally neglected.

The therapist often offers a secure attachment as a base from which to explore internal conflicts. Sometimes they might even offer the first experience of a secure attachment that the client has ever encountered. Our need to attach is not in question. Our ability to attach, however, is often moulded in a way that means we may not be able to access our true potential and the life we want to live. We all have gifts and must be courageous enough to step into our own power to discover them. Elsa's power of cryokinesis is pretty spectacular, and while we might not all be able to create ice mountains with our mind every one of us possesses of our own unique gifts. In childhood, the nature and location of those gifts within us can become obscured and lost if we have learnt to attach in ways that involve hiding parts of ourselves.

Exercises

1. Which attachment styles resonate with you the most?
2. Can you identify behaviours in your relationships that might be self-limiting and causing difficulties that could relate to attachment styles?
3. Growing up, did you experience secure attachments? Did you experience anxious, avoidant or disorganised attachments? With who?

References

Ainsworth, M. D. S. and Bell, S. M. (1970). Attachment, exploration, and separation: Illustrated by the behavior of one-year-olds in a strange situation. Child Development, 41(1), 49–67. https://doi.org/10.2307/1127388

Bowlby, J. (1969). *Attachment and Loss: Attachment Volume 1*. London: Penguin.

Main, M. and Solomon, J. (1990). Procedures for identifying infants as disorganized/disoriented during the Ainsworth strange situation. In: *Attachment in the Preschool Years* (ed. M.T. Greenberg, D. Cicchetti, and E.M. Cummings), 121–160. Chicago: University of Chicago Press.

13

Scripts and *Poor Things*

Theory: Scripts

This is the psychological theory that we live our lives using a narrative known as a script which unconsciously dictates decisions we make. We have characters, plot and setting, just like a film script, but these scripts are written when we are very young children, where we only have access to basic systems of emotional understanding (Berne 1961).

Movie: *Poor Things (2023)*

Victoria Blessington, a married, pregnant woman, commits suicide by jumping off a bridge, but is brought back to life by Godwin, a maverick scientist, who removes the brain of the foetus and implants it into Victoria. He renames her Bella Baxter. Bella outperforms all Godwin's expectations, and her insatiable curiosity and zest for life challenge Godwin's ideas of love and loss, nature and nurture. Adapted from the book of the same name by Alasdair Grey, *Poor Things*, directed by Yorgos Lanthimos, is Frankenstein reimagined in the realm of the fantastic. Bella is learning about the world through an infant mind in her woman's body. Godwin, referred to by Bella as God, asks Max McCandles, a brilliant medical student, to document Bella's progress, which is '*advancing at speed.*' Bella becomes betrothed to Max but takes off with the wealthy Duncan Wedderburn to '*adventure before marriage.*' Wedderburn is as mesmerised with the simple novelty of Bella as he is blind to her true complexity and, despite his best efforts, cannot make her conform to his will. Bella returns to God when she learns of his ill-health and, in turn, discovers the truth about her former life, including her husband, General Alfie Blessington, who arrives to claim the woman he knew as Victoria Blessington. Bella must make a choice between her old life/self and her new one.

What We're Doing

In this chapter, we will be looking at the psychological theory of scripts through the eyes of the main character, Bella Baxter, in the movie *Poor Things*. As we learn about script theory, we will use it to understand and explore Bella's needs, her drives and her values. Using my own experience in training, I invite you to consider how the theory may relate to your life.

Eric Berne discussed six types of script: Until, After, Never, Always, Almost and Open End, with each type of script having its own specific limitations and permissions (Berne 1970).

Let's explore scripts (Stewart and Jones 1978) through what Godwin might say:

'*I won't think about fun **until** I've brought this dead woman back to life.*' But in truth, after Bella, Godwin will find something else that is of utmost importance before he can be present in his life. He cannot actually live and develop the other parts of himself **until** he finds the elusive something else and it is this **Until** which keeps him unknowingly stuck in his script.

'*After Bella, my most marvelous creation, nothing else can ever compare.*' There is a sense here that there will be a cost to achieving what he wants and it will be paid **after** the moment of fullness arrives. It is this **After** which keeps him unknowingly stuck in his script, battling with a sense of meaninglessness and impending disappointment that life cannot ever live up to his expectations.

'*Bella will **never** be anything but an experiment.*' The **Never** script has a pessimistic finality to it. It obliterates all other possibilities and the limitations it presents are a reflection of how Godwin sees himself and his own abilities in life. Godwin unconsciously believes he will **never** be enough and it is this **Never** which keeps him unknowingly stuck in his script.

'*I have **always** been a man that must choose between science or human connection.*' The **Always** script provides a rational excuse for avoiding emotional risks. It is also the other end of **Never** in terms of absolutes. Godwin must **always** behave in a certain way, creating the same limitations as in the **Never** script but in a less overt manner because the emphasis is on doing rather than not doing. It is the act of **always** having to repeat a certain behaviour which rules out the option of freedom to consider other choices and it is this **Always** which keeps him unknowingly stuck in his script.

'*I **almost** made it into the scientific hall of fame.*' Godwin is unlikely to be publicly rewarded for his scientific brilliance in human reanimation. However, without the scientific community's validation, it is hard for him to truly celebrate his achievements and forge a sense of self-worth. Godwin is consigned to an endless search for approval and achievement, but only ever **almost** attaining it, and he struggles to reach a place of contentment in his own life or a true appreciation for the self. It is this **Almost** which keeps him unknowingly stuck in his script.

'*Without Bella, there is nothing.*' In the **Open-ended** script, there is a specific moment where the cosmic vastness of life has taken over and there is nothing more to see or do. There is no fatigue, as in the **Until** or **Always** script, the constant need to do before contentment can be had. There is no slim hope, as contained in the **Almost** script, or the pessimism of the **Never** script. There is no fear, as attached to the **After** script. What we do have is a void, an emptiness, a nothing and so the **Open-ended** script is lived with the existential dread of this existential nothing underlying every action.

Whenever you hear people say, '*that's ridiculous*' about a movie, it is normally because something unbelievable has happened in the script and the audience does not or cannot believe it. Human beings are a potent dichotomy of both change and stuckness. Imagination and reality. We watch movies searching for commonality and resonance, often to find a place we recognise from which we can then escape. Life scripts are not that different. They are not written cognitively by adults on computers or paper, but unconsciously by children who embody them in body memories. Children organise their script beliefs into little filing cabinets that they then forget about, but continue to pull files from in adulthood to help them live their lives. Once we can understand the life script we wrote as children, we can then become aware of the nature of certain script messages and know the places in our personal story where we feel stuck. The places that feel scary and from which we attempt to escape. In therapy we look at these script messages through closer examination, exploring the drama triangle, Drivers, attachment styles, strokes, transactions, Hungers, and our own Parent, Adult and Child ego states. In *Poor Things*, Bella is in an interesting position because she is a child writing her life script while at the same time being an adult who is rewriting her life script. This is the true brilliance of Godwin's creation: a human who can fall at the same time as she gets up, who can hurt at the same time as she loves, who can bleed at the same time as she heals.

When I moved to my new training institute, I started to receive some script messages that were confusing. Contrary to my educational life up to that point, I was now being told I was thriving academically and being encouraged to do more to find my voice. I started to write a regular 'Film Scripts' column for the *Transactional Analysis Journal*, where I psychoanalysed films and television programmes. I could feel and see how, in writing this column about scripts (unbeknownst to me, the embryo for the book you are now reading), I was starting to rewrite my own life script. An old script reinforced by parents, teachers, relationships, environment, culture, class, race, politics, sex and last but by no means least, personality, was being overlaid with a new script. I was no longer defining my reality to justify my script, but I was creating a new reality that could no longer justify an old, outdated script. The first time I saw my name and column in print, I could feel how my script lived in my body. I felt nervous and scared, as if I was doing something wrong. I also felt excited and quietly thrilled that my thoughts and words were being witnessed. I also felt sad that this part of me had been hidden away for so long, wanting to be seen but scared of judgment and rejection. Berne talks about there always being a payoff at the end of the script. A script payoff is the final scene, the culmination and unconsciously decided outcome that the child wrote before the age of seven about how it was all going to end and which the adult unconsciously tries to make happen. The training confronted me with my old script payoff – there is no happy ending for me.

Godwin did not tell Bella the truth about her origins. He created a fantasy that her parents were his friends, intrepid explorers, who died and he was left to look after baby Bella. Hearing this story, Bella shows empathy towards herself and self-compassion as she reflects, '*Poor Bella.*' She sees Godwin as her father and believes that her 'God' is loving and wants her to have the life that she wants. Godwin reads her stories and kisses her goodbye and, like the child she is, she feels loved and safe. Initially, her walk is unstable, like a baby's. She delights, as a toddler would, in spinning around and when she exclaims '*Weeee*,' Max assumes she is excited, surprised to then see a grown woman in a beautiful dress urinating on the floor.

As Bella grows, she takes in messages that help her write her script. The most important of these is that her parents were explorers and to push the boundaries as they did was, as Godwin informed her, '*the only way to live.*' Despite Bella being a child, this forms her blueprint for life, her script.

Bella is learning at an accelerated rate. She has a Hurry Up Driver (Chapter 7) with a secondary Try Hard Driver. Bella soon learns that the world is bigger than her house and filled with many different places and people. She tells Godwin that she wants to go out and he replies, '*So many things outside can kill you Bella. . .snakes, carriages, sharp-faced birds, earthquakes, inhalation of toxic grass seeds.*' Godwin's own father was a maverick scientist just like him and when Godwin relays stories of his childhood, Max is shocked that Godwin has endured behaviour that Max thinks of as cruel but which Godwin has gone on to normalise. When Max asks what there is to be gained from putting such fear onto Bella, Godwin says that Bella is his experiment, which means he must control the conditions. However, Godwin also admits to feeling paternal towards her in a way his own father never was to him. He speaks of the divide between science and feeling, the head and the heart and that his father sacrificed feeling for science – this is Godwin's script message. In his relationship with Bella, Godwin has surprised himself by doing both, doing something his father was unable to do.

Hearing Godwin say she cannot go out into the world, Bella becomes angry, smashing plates and screaming. She also withdraws, as a reaction to Godwin's attempt at controlling her. She resists succumbing to the fear that Godwin tries to coddle her with, breaking out of her physical and emotional body, '*You hold Bella too tight*,' she tells Godwin, who is attempting to give Bella the Don't Leave Me injunction (Chapter 15). Godwin chloroforms Bella. The morning she discovers she has been forcibly denied the pleasure she seeks externally, she learns to masturbate and give pleasure to herself internally. She learns on her voyage of sexual self-discovery that, '*in polite society, that is not done*.' Bella feels stuck in her script and is confused that something that feels good is deemed bad. *Poor Things* has at its heart the relationship between Bella and her own innocence versus the shame of the world. Bella continues to be thrilled and disappointed with her exploration of the world, as her infant mind demands she exorcise shame from her adult experience or at the very least, try to understand its purpose.

As Bella grows into her adolescence, she rebels against the status quo of society and Godwin's values, a psychologically vital aspect of her healthy emotional development. Godwin suggests that Max and Bella marry, which Bella agrees to, but also insists that they live with him in the family home. Duncan Wedderburn, a lawyer, is asked to draw up a legal agreement stating the terms of the betrothal. He sees Bella and is mesmerised; '*Something in you, some hungry being, hungry for experience, freedom, touch*.' Bella puts her plans to marry Max on hold to 'adventure' with Wedderburn. She shows her Stimulus Hunger (Chapter 5) as she tastes Portuguese custard tarts for the first time, gorges on them and then vomits. Her Incident Hunger emerges as she delights in watching Wedderburn about to throw her new friend, Martha, into the sea. We see her Contact Hunger satisfied when she asks Godwin to lie down in the bed and be near her as she sleeps. Her Recognition Hunger is exemplified when she starts working in a brothel and feels compelled to fight for a better work environment for herself and her friends. Her Sexual Hunger is satiated in her physical cravings for Wedderburn. And her Structure Hunger is fulfilled in the decision to study while working at the brothel.

Bella asks Godwin to allow her to be free. She rejects his Don't Be Important injunction. '*Kiss me and set me forth. If you do not, Bella's insides shall turn rotten with hate*.' Bella's speech is the inimitable formula of veracious innocence and mature wisdom. By asking for him to kiss her and set her forth, she acknowledges a complex script reality that without her father's blessing or permission to live her life by her own choices, her script could risk being dominated by a damaging love/hate parental relationship where she is unnaturally bound to a parent/family/culture and finds it hard to be happy and make decisions which fulfil her potential – a quandary faced by many in the real world. Bella travels the world. She learns about love, sex, capitalism, socialism, religion, poverty, class, feminism, philosophy, realism and hope and through it all she learns about herself. Godwin encourages Bella to hide away her differences from other people, offering her the Don't Belong injunction. Even though Wedderburn takes her out into society, he tells her what to say, attempting to give the Don't Be You injunction, trying also to offer her the Don't Think injunction – *'you're always reading now, Bella, you're losing some of your adorable way of speaking.'*

Bella learns about who she is, about what she wants, which is not to be shamed or controlled by others. She learns about the cruelty that exists within human beings in this world and her own powerlessness in response to it. She also learns about power and how to say 'no', to set boundaries for herself in adulthood that she did not learn as a child. Learning about her script messages is a slow journey for Bella rather than a lightbulb moment of existential understanding – exactly like us in the therapy room. Bella describes herself as a *'flawed, experimenting person'* – exactly like us in life.

Bella asks Wedderburn to assist her with empirical evidence to confirm whether she might be in love with him. Having started to feel empty during her time working as a prostitute in the brothel, Bella begins asking her clients to share a childhood memory in return for her telling them a joke. Despite her reanimated origins and the symbolism of her being created in the image of a monster, Bella intuitively understands the connection between the physical and the emotional and how script messages are stored in the body. She is attempting to emotionally connect with her clients to cope with the feeling of emptiness. Madame Swiney, who runs the brothel, tells Bella, *'knowing all the world in all its savage glory and this makes us whole.'* Swiney speaks of the parts of our script people might choose to ignore or not explore because they are painful, and that in facing ourselves, we have the opportunity to integrate consciously in a way that is holistically whole and representative of the human condition in its entirety.

> *You're in the dark period, before light and wisdom come to you. You must forge through it and once on the other side you will be grateful to this moment but you must keep going.*

Despite her encouragement of women advancing their position, Madame Swiney gives contradictory messages in the form of a Don't Succeed injunction when Bella tries to improve practices in the brothel. This frustrates Bella, who starts to rewrite her script in the face of similar limitations to those she faced with Godwin.

When Bella learns that God is dying, she returns home and asks Max to marry her. Bella has learned about what she loves and what interests her and has decided to become a doctor. Bella was given the extraordinary gift of life and desires to learn as a doctor how to cure the ills of those living ordinary lives. Godwin transplanting Bella's own baby's brain into her body is the metaphorical nexus of therapy as we strive to become our own loving parents to our own inner child.

BELLA: *Do you think people are improvable?*
MAX: *Just as a human body can be cured of illness, men and women can be cured of aspect.*

Bella and Max are interrupted at their wedding by the arrival of Bella's former husband, General Alfie Blessington. Bella learns details of her previous life and the tragic depths of her own former unhappiness. She learns about her former self, Victoria, in a way we might in therapy learn about parts of ourselves we have split off or chosen to ignore. Alfie's arrival shocks Bella and we see her begin her final explorations of the movie: male tyranny, patriarchal violence and the fear of women. Bella becomes a student of science and philosophy and chooses to write a new script.

Many parental and cultural script messages restrict the Child ego state's individual script, and later the Adult ego state's freedom. Despite Bella's biological challenges or perhaps indeed as a result of them, she has an intolerance and subsequent absence of shame. Combining this with her ability to be vulnerable and undefended, Bella has avoided playing emotional and psychological games with others. Despite being viewed as a monster, she is the only character in the movie who has avoided stepping onto the drama triangle (Chapter 6). It is perhaps only when we give attention to our monstrous parts that we can free ourselves from the shame of needing to hide them.

A common element in script messaging is fear. Godwin experienced fear of abandonment, fear of change, fear of difference, fear of feeling, fear of illness and fear of death. However, despite his real and sincere love for Bella, her own true happiness depended on her rejecting Godwin's script messages and challenging her own script.

I feel drawn to this word, 'shame.' It feels like no matter the theory, all roads lead back to shame. Witnessing Bella escape so many of the psychological pitfalls of human interaction, I can't help thinking that shame has a lot to answer for. But there is also something else here, something that I was unaware of on that first day of my training, and that is loss. I start to wonder about the relationship between shame and loss. And whether we might use shame to soften the pain of loss.

Exercises

1. Identify your script messages. Where might you be stuck in your script?
2. Now go a bit deeper. Which script messages feel good and which feel bad? Try going as far back as you can remember. Are there any that feel familiar but may be no longer needed? Are there any that feel scary but could be physically or emotionally healthy?
3. Give your life a movie title? Is this the movie you want to be in for the rest of your life or would you like to work on renaming it and on changing your script?

References

Berne, E. (1970). Sex In Human Loving. Simon and Schuster, New York.

Berne, E. (1961). *Transactional Analysis in Psychotherapy: A Systematic Individual and Social Psychiatry*. New York: Grove Press.

Stewart, I. and Joines, V. (1978). *TA Today: An Introduction to Transactional Analysis*. Nottingham and Chapel Hill: Lifespace Publishing.

14

Cultural Script and *Get Out*

Theory: Cultural Script

This is a psychological theory which refers to the unconscious behaviours, thoughts and assumptions created and dictated by a specific culture, including that of past generations and ancestral legacies (Drego 1996), which becomes enmeshed in a person's life script (Berne 1961).

Movie: *Get Out (2017)*

Chris, a young Black photographer, accompanies his White girlfriend, Rose Armitage, to meet her parents. Chris asks Rose if she has told her parents she is dating a Black man and that given he is the first Black man she has dated, maybe they should know. Rose finds this question redundant, assuring Chris, '*they are not racist. I would have told you.*' Chris and Rose arrive at the Armitage family home and a series of definitive, yet disorientingly insidious racist encounters ensue. Chris realises that Rose has been lying to him and that her family is part of a secret cult where her psychiatrist mother, Missy, hypnotises Black people to subdue and imprison them so that her neurosurgeon father, Dean, can lobotomise them, and implant their brains inside the mind of a White person. By the time Chris has discovered what the Armitage family are all about, he is in terrible danger.

What We're Doing

In this chapter, we will be looking at the cultural script through the movie *Get Out* and its main character, Chris. As we learn about cultural script theory, we will use it to understand and explore Chris' relationship to his

internal and external worlds. Using my own experience in training, I invite
you to consider how the theory may relate to your life.

In my training, there was me, one other Asian woman and one Black man;
the rest of the class was White. Born and raised in England, being the only
Asian woman in the room isn't something new to me. Most times, I do not
even notice, I am so used to ignoring my own skin colour and how my skin
looks contrasted against the backdrop of the White world around me. So used
to making myself presentable, my skin colour is obscured behind the oppression of racial hegemony. And yet, my cultural frame of reference is an integral
part of my individual frame of reference. How I see the world and how the
world sees me form these frames of reference, including how I have grown up
with physical and emotional experiences of my birth country's dominant
culture, deeming my inherited culture and that of my parents as inferior.

What do I mean by frame of reference? Let's consider this frame like the
actual frame of a painting. Different colours, different materials, different
widths – all change the way the picture looks inside. We all have our own
frame through which we see the picture that is our life. Experiences, personality and family create our frame and alter how we see the picture. We
have individual frames and our cultural script is sometimes the largest
part.

In *Get Out*, the first scene of the film opens in the dark. What is
obscured? Our eyes search the frame and we see a Black man, Andre, walking alone down the street. The first words spoken in the movie, Andre says,
'*What kind of sick individual. . .*' This sets the tone. In the shadowy romantic lighting of a tree-lined street, an apparently peaceful suburban neighbourhood, these words deliberately and jarringly pose a question. Andre
feels like he '*sticks out like a sore thumb*,' referring to his Blackness in this
White, affluent neighbourhood. A sports car drives past, slows, does a
U-turn and drives alongside the curb just behind him. The vaudeville theatre song 'Run Rabbit Run' plays out of lowered windows. The song, composed by Gay and Butler and first performed in 1939, at the start of the
Second World War, is about a farmer hunting and killing rabbits to make a
pie. The song, played out of context from a sports car with tinted windows
in 2017, conjures chilling historical similarities to the hunting of people.
Andre is attacked. We begin to get the idea that director Jordan Peele wants
us to question our normativity. The incongruity is not that Andre is a Black
man walking through a White neighbourhood, but how this manicured
White neighbourhood is so unsafe that Andre leaves it unconscious and in
the trunk of a car.

*What white people have to do is try and find out in their own hearts why it
is necessary to have a 'nigger' in the first place, because I am not a nigger, I'm
a man. But if you think I'm a nigger, it means you need him* – James Baldwin.

This quote from James Baldwin (Baldwin 2016) exemplifies the dehumanisation within the cultural script. Parts of the person are accepted and admired, and the very same parts, branded and brutalised.

In the next scene, we are introduced to Chris. He is shaving, making himself presentable. In a medium close-up, Rose is smiling, looking through the glass screen of a patisserie. Immediately, we associate Rose, and not merely because of her name, with sweetness, comfort and warmth. Rose arrives at the apartment and Chris opens the door. Without words, he pulls her towards him and they kiss. What do we assume about the other? When children come into this world, they are born into systems: family systems, historical systems and cultural systems. People grow from birth, operating on assumptions of pre-existing orders. Chris and Rose are instinctively and physically attracted to each other but what do they know or assume they know about each other's individual and cultural frames of reference?

Director Peele continues to offer juxtapositions within the narrative. A deer jumps frantically into the air and is hit by Rose's car. Rose and Chris are shocked and distressed by the ominous and prophetic incident but Chris is pacified watching Rose challenge a police officer on racial inequality. The officer asks to see Chris' ID despite Chris not being the driver. In reality, Rose is merely attempting to prevent Chris' identity from entering the system, so her family can lobotomise him and have him disappear from society without recourse. The chilling truth of her protest is unknown at this point. Chris says to Rose, '*that was hot.*'

The subservience that is encouraged and witnessed from Black men towards White law enforcement is rooted entirely in survival. It requires Chris to demonstrate inappropriate levels of compliance in the face of inequality as a legitimate form of self-protection. Chris' cultural need for protection originates and exists today within multiple systems: law, education, media, politics. Chris' cultural frame of reference will have not only incorporated these historic abuses but he will have developed strategies to survive these modern-day abuses. When Rose squares up to the police officer, Chris is enamoured. Here, his cultural frame of reference includes both being abused by the White man and grateful to the White woman. Chris' cultural lack of autonomy creates a contaminated relational co-dependence which sits unconsciously underneath his attraction to Rose.

The couple arrive at the family home. Dean insists Chris call him by his first name rather than '*Mr Armitage*', telling Chris that he and Missy are '*huggers.*' Such warm familial informality is contrasted as Peele pulls out into a long shot: a faceless Black man on the edge of the frame watches the house, threatening musical tones play out. Part of the cultural script includes the impact of marginalisation, where cultural minorities exist at the margins of society and become detached from their own sense of self.

Dean gives Chris a tour of the house, including all the artefacts he has brought back from his travels – '*it's such a privilege to be able to experience another person's culture.'* Dean tells Chris the story of his grandfather, Roman Armitage, beaten by Jesse Owens in the qualifying round for the 1936 Olympics, the games where Owens won in front of Hitler. Dean seems chuffed that a Black man is able to excel in the face of Hitler and his '*Aryan bullshit.'* Next come throwaway comments about the basement being sealed because of black mould and about Dean allowing the workforce that served his parents to stay on because he wants to keep a piece of his mother in the kitchen. At this point, Chris is unaware that Dean's mother's brain has been implanted in the skull of the lobotomised Georgina, the Black housemaid. We pan to Georgina and in Peele's fine blend of dialogue and camera, he begins to construct Dean's cultural frame of reference for us.

Indeed, Roman Armitage did not ever get over being beaten by a Black man and, in reaction to his shame, confusion, sadness and anger, he formed the '*Order of the Coagula,'* a secret cult. Dean tells Chris that he knows how it looks, '*White family, Black servants.'* That it must seem like a '*total cliche.'* Dean does not see that the real cliche, and what truly betrays a lack of original thought, is telling Chris that he would have voted for Obama for a third term. Dean's reliance on social category thinking (Liberman et al. 2017) is in part due to America's history and how long it has taken for a non-White president to come into office. Dean assumes, simplistically, that because Obama is Black, Chris would have voted for him, and also that Chris would be pleased to know that Dean voted for him. He also assumes that Chris will use this knowledge to counteract the moral optics of Dean having Black servants. Placing people into social categories helps us both make meaning and connect to each other. Dean is trying to make meaning and connect with Chris to lull him into a false sense of security. When social category thinking goes too far, it begins to mask a fear. Chris can sense something isn't right, but has no idea how deep the Armitage fear goes.

As the movie continues, we see Chris pushed and pulled between knowing in his gut that something is terribly wrong, but sticking with the situation. Take the anodyne and robotic Stepford-wife-esque Georgina (NB: the original 1975 *The Stepford Wives* movie was one of Peele's influences). Chris knows that her level of servitude is far from normal, but what seems even more concerning is how a part of Georgina's self/identity appears as if it is trying to break free but is locked inside. Peele's depiction of the staff who have had transplants, Black on the outside but White consciousness on the inside, is the psychological illustration of a cultural frame of reference where a person feels forced to lock up a part of themselves to be better and more safely accepted in wider society. The parallels to locked-in syndrome, the neurological condition where a person is conscious but physically paralysed and unable to communicate verbally, are frighteningly redolent of racism and cultural subjugation. When Missy taps her spoon against a teacup, a hypnosis-conditioned stimulus, Georgina is immediately reminded of the small conscious part of her which still remains after the implant, and her eyes fill with tears.

Looking around the room at my training institute, I see the other Asian woman and the Black man sitting in a sea of White people. How do I reconcile why people tan to darken their skin, but would rather my brown arm not brush against them in a queue? Why are people happy to donate to charities in Africa but are shocked when a dark-skinned girl is brought home for dinner? To fit in, I have had to lock my colour away but there are moments on the course that I feel my locked-away parts unexpectedly emerge. Like the Black characters in the movie, I am taken back to the many times in my life when I have heard jokes I did not find funny, and a forced, locked-in Stepford-esque smile arrived on my face, but not in my eyes.

At the family dinner, we meet Jeremy, Rose's brother. '*With your frame and your genetic make-up,*' Jeremy leans into Chris, eyes narrowed, ramping up the intensity of his inquisition of his sister's boyfriend, '*if you really pushed your body, really trained, no pussyfooting around, you'd be a fucking beast.*' The flattery is overtly sadistic, the subject is sport. Predictable, casual even, and yet there is something both blatantly unhinged and yet somehow hard to identify in his provocative and jovial demeanour. It is easy to assume that Chris is simply choosing to diplomatically avoid reacting to his new girlfriend's pretentious brother. But how are Rose and Dean able to keep quiet? What is the nature of Rose's cultural frame of reference that she has inherited from her family?

Rose feigns surprise that the weekend she and Chris are visiting her parents has coincided with the big annual family get-together. Dean explains how the tradition, started by Rose's grandfather Roman, has continued to keep '*them close to us.*' He explains here the essence of the cultural script; how it is born but also survives. The truth of this comment cannot be overstated, as implanting the mind of his mother into Georgina and that of his father into Walter is the heinous epitome of cultural scripting. Often, cultural scripting is stronger and more pervasive than the individual's own script, as it is composed of many voices and trans-generational scripts which are condensed and compressed. Dean preserves the White supremacist ideology from his father by literally keeping the legacy alive, immaculately preserving and continuing trans-generational trauma.

Missy and Dean take issue with Chris' '*nasty habit*' of smoking. Their evil is disguised by a thin veil of normality/normativity and they use the psychological device of projection by referencing a societal vice. Ostensibly, to help Chris quit, Missy hypnotises him. It is here that he enters the '*sunken place,*' an existential blackness of complete fear and isolation within the mind. Being in the sunken place has the same feel for Chris as the locked-in-syndrome-esque terror, randomly experienced by Georgina and Walter when they momentarily become aware of their predicament. Chris can see but he cannot touch. He is aware of falling but he does not reach any point of arrival. It is a constant freefall into a state of indefinite terror whilst being conscious but powerless. All these feelings are part of the cultural script and, in particular, the cultural shadow (Drego 1996), a part of the cultural script Drego located in the Child ego state. The cultural shadow can be activated unconsciously by others, just as Missy is activating it through her hypnotism.

Chris starts taking photos at the Armitages' annual party. Peele uses Chris' photography to allow the audience a snapshot of what is really in the frame. The director's choices echo a camera obscura (which inverts and reverses a picture), confronting the audience with a reality distorted by Chris' own cultural script as well as the cultural scripting which exists in society. The whole movie is a grotesque unpeeling of the fear and evil that resides within humanity. Rose's cultural script joins together with Chris' to form a cultural enmeshment; they can no longer identify or honour their own value systems and so become pawns of what they have inherited and what has been passed down. Chris meets Jim Hudson, the owner of Hudson Galleries, a blind art dealer who is familiar with and likes Chris' work, having described it at the party as '*brutal*' and '*melancholy*'. Jim 'wins' Chris in what seems like a game, but transpires to be an actual silent human auction. Jim asks Chris not to tar him with the opinions of the lesser racists, who covet Chris for his physical body alone. He feels his desire is for 'something deeper' – Chris' eyesight. Jim legitimises Chris' imprisonment and impending lobotomy and feels that this justification sets him apart. Jim needs and wants to see the world the way Chris does in all its colour and believes that winning Chris and owning his eyes would give him an ethical superiority over the other cult members. That his personal goal goes beyond colour prejudice and in that way, he does not see colour. Jim is double blind to the fact that to possess Chris' eyesight, Jim seeks assistance from a cult rooted in a specific cultural scripting; fear-driven, prejudicial and using hierarchical tyranny and oppression to deem one race superior to another. Chris simply exists as parts to be split off, dissected, stripping him of any dignity as a human. Jim fails to understand that for him to see the world the way Chris does he must also have had to endure the racism Chris has and experienced how the body and sight changes when it is subject to ongoing brutal melancholia.

As more guests arrive at the party, microaggressions move from being couched in familial rhetoric to becoming vulgar and obvious. '*I do know Tiger,*' Gordon, one of the guests, says to Chris, referring to Black golfer Tiger Woods. Lisa, another guest, lusts over Chris, '*how handsome is he?*' She squeezes his biceps and strokes his pecs; Chris remains still, objectified. She asks Rose, '*Is it true? Is it better?*' referring to having sex with a Black man. Another couple, '*Fairer skin has been in favour for the last couple of hundred of years but now the pendulum has swung back, Black is in fashion.*' During all these encounters, Chris is polite, non-defensive and silent.

Chris spots Andre at the party and greets him. However, like with Georgina and Walter, there is something missing in the eyes. Chris focuses on the comments of the two Black staff rather than commenting on the last three shockingly racist comments made to him by Rose's family friends. '*It's not what he says, it's how he says it,*' says Chris, describing Walter, one of the lobotomised Black staff, as hostile. Rose's whole family, however, have been given a free pass. Why is their more refined brand of hostility more acceptable to Chris? Is it because they are White, related to Rose and occupy a certain place in society? Chris guesses that Walter is hostile because he might not like the fact that Chris and Rose are together. He is right. The White, older minds inside Georgina and Walter's bodies would not have approved of Chris and Rose's relationship. A Japanese man asks Chris if he feels that '*being Afro American has more advantage or disadvantage in the modern world?*' Chris throws the question to Andre, the only other Black guest at the party. Chris assumes that Andre, as a Black man, will have a desire or ability to answer. Social category thinking and Chris' desperate need for protection are what facilitate the search for an ally in Andre as he starts to feel the isolation and alienation of the 'sunken place.' He takes a photo but the flash triggers something in Andre, who starts to bleed from his nose whilst aggressively demanding that Chris '*Get out!*' This is a warning that Chris must physically get out of the Armitage house and family but also emotionally get out of his cultural script.

Chris tells Rose he wants to leave. Rose appears sad that he might leave without her. Despite Peele's sociopathic presentation of Rose, cultural scripting can place a huge strain on a relationship. Rose manipulates Chris, keeping her family's cultural script alive and fuelling the couple's cultural enmeshment. Chris is hypnotised and strapped to a chair as Dean preps for the implant operation. Chris knows he must '*get out,*' further confirmed by a video he is played of the late Roman Armitage talking about the '*physical advantages*' of the Black race, their '*natural gifts*' being merged with the '*determination*' of the White race so that they can '*both be part of something greater, something perfect.*' Chris discovers that Rose has lured other Black men before Chris to the house to be lobotomised. Despite the fact that Chris was her '*favourite,*' she is still adapting to her grandfather's script. Roman created the Order of the Coagula to conceal his own insecurities and project his own anger and fear, using a pre-existing order firmly established in the world by racism. The Armitage cultural script of ethnic cleansing has been dressed up in medical advancement to hide what is a primal fear of the other and fear of the self.

Chris escapes by stuffing his ears with padding from the chair he sits in, which blocks out the attempts to hypnotise him. The cultural script is so strong that to resist its influence, we often need to find a way to stop listening; the unconscious impact of what we are absorbing is as powerful as being hypnotised.

The diagram below (Fig. 14.1) illustrates negative symptoms of cultural scripting. As human beings, our understanding of the world and the meaning we attach to it is interwoven into our survival and, as such, our identity. Being part of a cultural group means that we belong, we are protected and we survive. It is the cultural script that allows for a powerful feeling of belonging and there can be a confusing and incredibly painful sense of alienation when we break free from it. However, in remaining bound to it we can also experience alienation from our true selves. The members of the culture place a huge emotional and psychological pressure, verbal and non-verbal, on Chris to conform, which can feel suffocating. Chris becomes objectified, his own identity dispensed with as the Coagula tries to 'make him White': forced cultural appropriation. Think of the camera obscura - this is when light projects a reversed and inverted image. 'Obscura' derives from the Latin word for shadowy and dark - cultural script theory helps us understand that it is in the obscura that it becomes hard to see the shadow. A camera obscura of sorts takes Rose's and Chris' individual scripts and their cultural enmeshment, distorts and reflects, and creates what I like to call a "Cultural Obscura".

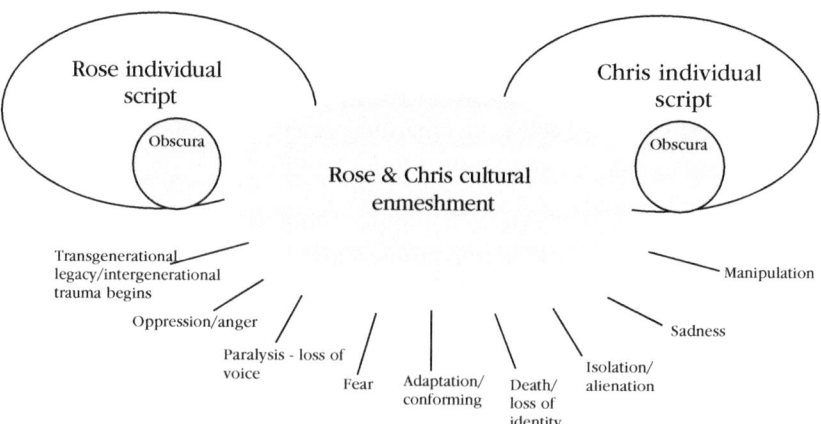

Fig. 14.1   Cultural Obscura

Peele shows Rose sitting on her bed with her headphones on, multicoloured cereal loops in one bowl, white milk in another; she cannot hear and is oblivious to the deaths of her family members happening all around her, and is portrayed like an impressionable teenager in her own world searching the internet for her new boyfriend/the family's next target.

Allowing fear to drive us means we must split off parts of ourselves to obscure what we do not want to see. Terrified, we diminish our true selves and hide in the dark. The alternative is understanding and honouring our own complex cultural identity. Only then can we decide exactly what parts of our cultural script we want to change.

Exercises

1. Make a list of all the cultural values that exist for your parents.
2. Assess if any of these particular values are causing you to struggle in your present life. Which are theirs, which are yours and which are shared?
3. Could you be in a cultural enmeshment with anyone in your family or your partner and what is in your obscura which may be causing a cultural enmeshment?

References

Baldwin, J. (2016). I Am Not Your Negro [film]. Directed by R. Peck.

Berne, E. (1961). *Transactional Analysis in Psychotherapy: A Systematic Individual and Social Psychiatry*. New York: Grove Press.

Drego. P. (1996) Cultural parent oppression and regeneration. Transactional Analysis Journal 26 (1), pg 58–77.

Liberman, Z., Woodward, A.L., and Kinzler, K.D. (2017). The origins of social categorization. *Trends in Cognitive Sciences Journal* 21 (7): 556–568. https://pubmed.ncbi.nlm.nih.gov/28499741 (accessed 16 September 2025).

15

Injunctions and *The Sound of Music*

Theory: Injunctions

The psychological theory of injunctions (Goulding and Goulding 1976) explains the unconscious messages children receive that inhibit their thoughts and behaviour. Injunctions involve a lack of permission and also an overcompensation.

Movie: *The Sound of Music (1965)*

Maria, a young nun, is sent by her Mother Superior to act as governess to a local family. The Reverend Mother is suspicious that Maria's sworn vocation as a nun may be a decision she has made with her head and not her whole heart. She insists Maria leave the nunnery and become a governess to seven children: Leisl, Friedrich, Louisa, Kurt, Brigitta, Marta and Gretl. Maria finds herself quite unexpectedly falling in love with widowed Captain von Trapp and facing the truth of her desire, acknowledging strong and ardent feelings she has tried to ignore in order to uphold the idea of who she thinks she should be.

What We're Doing

In this chapter, we will be looking at the psychological theory of injunctions in the movie, *The Sound of Music*. As we learn about injunctions, we will use them to understand and explore how the characters in the movie prohibit or limit themselves and their choices. Using my own experience in training, I invite you to consider how the theory may relate to your life.

There are many things I appreciated about my training. The opportunity to be with people who wanted to talk about their internal emotional struggles was probably the biggest one. Growing up in 80s London, I frequently felt as if I didn't belong. Did I belong in a country where I couldn't see any of the food I ate in my house in a supermarket or where I couldn't see anyone that looked like me on television or in magazines? Did I belong in my all-White school, the only Asian girl, the only girl subjected to the alienating and aggressive responses to my brown skin? Did I belong in my birth family, where I often felt misunderstood, as if I was getting it all wrong and just wasn't good enough? Where my mother felt I was too emotional and too prone to talking about emotions. Did I belong in a world that felt hard, as if it couldn't see the real me?

Maria is ashamed that the Reverend Mother wants to send her away, whilst the Reverend Mother believes Maria is running away from her feel-ings. Leaving the abbey feels like a punishment for Maria and she does not want to go but when she meets Captain von Trapp's children, she feels an immediate warmth for these young souls who have lost their mother and are in need of love and guidance. The Captain models various unconscious messages for the children: Don't Feel, Don't Think, Don't Touch and Don't Be Close. Their grief is not welcome in the house and there is no mention of their mother or the tragedy they have collectively shared. He separates himself from them, trapped in a prison of his own frozen sadness; their movement, their laughter, their life, only serving to remind him of what he has lost.

At the end of the second year, two monumental shifts occurred. The first was sitting for my diploma. I had been desperately nervous, to the point where I announced to my two examiners, 30 seconds after sitting down, that sometimes when I'm this nervous, I want to piss myself or cry. A leakage in the body or welcome relief? Both. Whispered voices in my head – 'Don't Succeed,' 'Don't Make It.' It transpired that just being able to say the fear out loud was all I needed, as after I made my disclosure, I felt calmer and an hour later I passed. And passed really well! It appeared that feeling and talking about emotions was what I needed to do and a world where that could happen was a world I understood. I had found a place. A place I had a particular affinity for and connection to and somewhere I belonged. What I didn't expect was that feeling a sense of belonging suddenly allowed me access to a deeper grief. It got me in touch with times I had known the pain of not belonging and the pain of suffocating hopelessness. Alongside this grief was also a happiness, as now it felt like there were possibilities. Life felt richer, airy and hopeful – I made a connection to myself and in doing that had somehow rooted myself in the world around me. It was as if a sign with the name of the place I had lived in for so long now looked different, the old name peeling away.

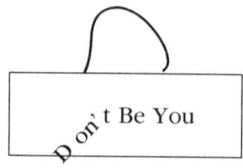

In that moment, something shifted and I registered to do a Master's in Psychotherapy. This was an idea I had previously entirely dismissed, believing that there was no way I could do it.

The second significant shift came during a class exercise. It was the end of the academic year and as a goodbye ritual, everyone took turns sitting in the hot seat. One by one, each member of the class was invited to offer their experience of the individual in the seat. Pagan, the tutor, asked us to try and avoid the compulsion to focus on being nice or flattering to the person, and to attempt a genuine and authentic connection. That only in the real and honest articulation of our experience of another person, could we offer a positive, unconditional stroke. This made me think about how often I feel a sense of disconnection in relationships. How often I want the connection between me and another person to feel more real than it does.

Despite the big band nervous drum roll that was building in my body, I started to wonder if this was the kind of meaningful connection I'd been missing. As the festivities progressed, the group started to get more comfortable with offering feedback. What at first feels startling moves towards the comfort of being truly seen and then to an intimacy in truly being noticed. I took my turn, settled into the seat and waited. My legs and my heart felt fizzy and light, not steady. Each person began by saying my name and took their turn to tell me about what they thought of me, how they experienced me, what I brought up for them emotionally. I could feel a slow trickle of numbness start to spread throughout my body. As the comments continued, I could hear the words but they did not reach me, falling before they could enter me and lying like letters on a doormat. Unopened. I waited until the last person had spoken and then ran out of the room in floods of tears, taking my shame with me.

Goulding and Goulding published the first group of injunctions, which they then went on to expand and which McNeel (2010) later added to. The easiest way to understand an injunction is as the opposite of a permission – things we learn not to be, feel or do. However, as injunctions are psychological messages that we receive in early childhood, they are predominantly non-verbal and at such an early age, we cannot remember the source of their formation or how we might have processed the information. Think of them as invisible military commanders. We listen and we obey, but we do not know we are being instructed. This is what can make injunctions difficult to identify. This means that we must be slow and careful investigators as we examine and pay attention to the evidence – what we feel and what we do – to be able to understand how we might be limiting ourselves in daily life without conscious awareness.

The Captain refers to clothing he wants the children to wear as '*uniforms*.' Maria refers to such clothing as '*straitjackets*.' He uses a whistle to call the children to him and each child has a different whistle command. Such an action depersonalises the children and by not using their names, he distances himself from having an emotional connection with them. Have you ever noticed how you might not use a person's name if you're angry with them or use their formal name rather than a name that evokes intimacy and happier times? Maria refuses to answer a whistle herself, saying *'whistles are for dogs and cats,'* and that it would be *'too humiliating.'* The Captain's response to Maria refusing to be humiliated is, *'Were you this much trouble at the abbey?'*

Maria refuses humiliation ⟹ Captain projects negative ⟹ Don't Be You

The Captain unconsciously models a Don't Trust. He cannot bear to show his vulnerability to his children, he does not trust that it will be okay. He demands that the children have a Don't Be Important so the children are forced to put their needs away, to bury them. A child is unable to emotionally understand the complexity of a parent being a flawed human. *'They love you too much, they fear you too much,'* Maria tells the Captain. Maria has observed the children and tells him how they have done their best but cannot simply remove their emotional needs because that's what he demands, that their needs will not just disappear. The Don't injunction has a child feeling that whatever they do is wrong. Maria has glimpsed some of the behaviours in the different personalities of the children. When the Captain protests her conclusions about the children, she answers, echoing what many couples therapists hear in their sessions, *'You're never home long enough to know.'* He cannot argue. The Captain has avoided spending time in the house. The memories of his late wife are too painful, his grief too overwhelming, so he shuns all emotional intimacy to avoid further pain. In fact, his new relationship with Baroness Schraeder appears to be a show of intimacy, but actually further helps to distract him as it remains superficial.

Kurt holds a Don't Feel, *'he pretends he's tough not to show how hurt he is when you push him aside,'* Maria tells the Captain. Friedrich holds a Don't Grow Up, *'he's a boy but wants to be a man like you and there's no one to show him how'* and Leisl holds a Don't Be Visible, *'not a child anymore, one of these days you're gonna wake up and find out she's a woman – you won't even know her.'* The Captain is not happy with Maria's forthright opinions on his parenting, but he cannot deny to himself that for the first time since his wife died, he feels seen and the connection feels real.

The Captain and the Baroness get engaged. At the same time, witnessing the changes in his family brought about by the influence of Maria, the Captain starts to soften his stance and is perturbed by the sensations he is starting to feel in himself. His desire to connect to his children returns. Even more problematic is the desire he has started to feel for Maria.

He realises that after his wife died, his relationship to joy had suffered and he was carrying a Don't Enjoy injunction. Despite their 'power couple' appearance and the lavish lifestyle the Captain leads with the Baroness, he still carries an emptiness. '*It's no use, you and I, I'm being dishonest to both of us,*' he tells the Baroness, who tells him to stop. She cannot bear to hear out loud the truth she has known for some time, that he does not love her and is in love with Maria (who he later goes on to marry).

In adulthood, we are still responding to childhood injunctions and it can be frightening to confront them. When we are honest about how limited we are and admit the limitations of the lives we are living, it can be incredibly painful. Why did I run away, I ask myself, hiding away in a toilet cubicle, fresh tears on my face? Hearing authentic comments from my peers and how they observed me, I felt completely seen, which felt overwhelming. To conceal my overwhelm and vulnerability from people, I had to escape. I returned to the group after some cathartic sobbing and explained the grief and shame that had come up from all the years of feeling unseen. The fear of feeling unsafe in a group. I had to challenge my Don't Relax, and really tolerate the uncomfortable feeling of being seen by others whilst recognising how, without it, I was reinforcing my Don't Belong. There was a sadness for my Child who had wanted something different for herself. Rammond (1994) writes about the script held by the child of an immigrant family and the Don't Change injunction that is offered. There is shame for me in having thoughts and opinions which are seen as challenging cultural norms: Don't Think.

The movie is set as the Second World War is breaking out. The Captain is faced with the changing face of Austria. He is ordered to take down the Austrian flag and replace it with the Nazi flag. The most threatening of all the injunctions is Don't Exist, the injunction forced upon any race or culture that is being persecuted and whose human rights are denied. The von Trapps enter a talent competition, knowing the soldiers will be distracted when the lights are down and the family will have a chance to disappear. Rather than be forced to be part of a war he does not agree with, the Captain plans a daring escape with his new wife, Maria, and the children as they give themselves permission to live the life they choose.

For the next goodbye ritual, I allowed the words from my fellow students to get right inside and I allowed the Don't to fall right off.

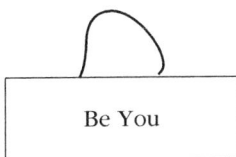

Be You

Exercises

1. Do any injunctions resonate with you? Can you think of any of your own?
2. Which experiences might have created these injunctions for you?
3. What would it be like to have the Don't part of your sign fall off? How different would your life look?

References

Goulding, R. and Goulding, M. (1976). Injunctions, decisions and redecisions. *Transactional Analysis Journal* 6 (1): 41–48.

McNeel, J.R. (2010). Understanding the power of injunctive messages and how they are resolved in redecision therapy. *Transactional Analysis Journal* 40 (2): 159–169.

Rammond, C. (1994). Don't change: a cultural injunction. *Transactional Analysis Journal* 24 (3): 22–221.

16

Projection and *Carrie*

Theory: Projection

The psychological theory of an uncomfortable emotion or feeling being unconsciously pushed away and projected onto another person.

Movie: *Carrie (1976)*

A shy, awkward teenage girl, physically and emotionally bullied by her mother, goes on to be bullied by her peers at school, the impact of which eventually culminates at a shocking and blood-filled prom where Carrie exacts her revenge.

What We're Doing?

In this chapter, we will be looking at the psychological theory of projection through Brian De Palma's seminal movie *Carrie*, through the eponymous lead character and those around her. As we learn about projection, we will develop a better understanding of Carrie's emotional world and her behaviours. Using my own experience in training, I invite you to consider how the theory may relate to your life.

The movie opens with a game of volleyball. Comments from the other girls like, '*we can't win a game with her on the team*,' introduce us to the main character, Carrie White. In an iconic scene, Carrie is terrified when she gets her period for the first time. She has no idea what is happening, as no one has ever discussed menstruation with her. The girls in the locker room mercilessly ridicule her, throwing tampons and period pads at her as Carrie crouches naked in the corner of the room, screaming and crying. A light bulb explodes, which appears at this point to be a coincidence but is actually a result of Carrie's telekinesis (the ability to move things with one's mind). Rita, the PE teacher, confirms to the headmaster that Carrie has always been the girls' '*scapegoat.*'

Salvador Minuchin (1974), an Argentinian psychotherapist, first introduced the term 'scapegoat' to explain a particular role often occupied by a child within a family. The purpose of the scapegoat in a family is to serve as a collective distraction to remove the acknowledgement and consequences of the family's dysfunction and also of personal parental accountability. Once the scapegoat has been selected, those close to and around the individual: siblings, extended family, teachers and peers tend to support the narrative. Projection is a defence mechanism that involves unconsciously ascribing your own feelings onto another person. When Rita describes Carrie as a scapegoat at the start of the movie, she foreshadows not only the projection from the other girls at school but also from Carrie's own mother.

Carrie as the scapegoat:

- Carrie behaves differently from '*the rest of us.*'
- Carrie is blamed by her mother.
- Carrie is seen as the problem.
- Carrie feels powerless.
- Carrie receives projections from others.

We discover that Mrs. White has a history of questionable parenting in Rita's eyes, with Rita disparagingly saying, '*knowing that mother of hers.*' The headmaster tells Rita that they cannot '*interfere with people's beliefs.*' However, Mrs. White, an ardent evangelist, chooses, because of her zealotry, to try to influence what other people believe, attempting to project her own beliefs onto them, as we were see her doing with. Mrs. Snell, the mother of Sue, one of the more popular girls at the school. Not condoning their behaviour, Rita does confess to understanding the other girls' frustration with Carrie, wanting to '*take her and shake her too. It was just her period, for God's sake.*' When Rita slaps Carrie in the shower, it is to shock Carrie out of her hysteria but Rita's earlier confession shows that she is also physically projecting her own frustration with the situation onto Carrie. The headmaster finds it hard to believe that Carrie knows nothing about her own period at her age, and we see how the person in charge of Carrie's pastoral wellbeing has no ability to see/understand what Carrie is going through at home. He shows and projects his confusion onto Carrie when he refers to her by an incorrect name, Cassie Wright. After hearing repeated incorrect versions of her name and quietly attempting to correct the headmaster, Carrie can bear it no longer and unconsciously projects her anger. She lets out an uncontrollable scream, at which point an ashtray spins into the air and smashes to the floor. Carrie let out the same scream in the shower, which resulted in the exploding light bulb. Carrie's screaming was the first moment in the movie that we see both her projecting the anger she was feeling and the consequences of her anger.

Learning about projection had me wondering about all the times I have unconsciously behaved in a way that might seem as if it is not about me when it was actually all about me, and how I cope with feelings that do not feel good inside me. Even the way I had come to view Bella, my first tutor, now felt like a projection. I had projected a nurturing mother role onto Bella and, though there were disappointments with Bella's behaviour over my placement, I wondered now if there was also something else underlying my feelings. I wondered whether the real disappointment was in my relationship with my own mother. When Bella fell off the Nurturing Parent pedestal I had put her on, had it activated an old yet all too familiar maternal disappointment? I started to get an inkling of how projection acts as a defence mechanism – how it keeps us safe…for a while.

When Carrie asks her mother why she didn't tell her about menstruation, Mrs. White slaps her. She starts reading passages from the Bible, '*Eve was weak and loosed the raven on the world, the raven was called Sin.*' She asks Carrie to repeat the words, '*the first sin was intercourse.*' Mrs. White kneels down, forcing Carrie to pray with her – '*show her that if she had remained sinless the curse of blood would never have come upon her.*' Carrie pleads that she has not done anything sinful but Mrs. White insists there must have been lustful thoughts and dragging her across the floor, she locks Carrie in the kitchen cupboard.

Mrs. White's reaction to Carrie's first period is drenched in her own shame and she uses the Bible to protect her secret shame and project it onto Carrie. When Carrie eventually emerges from the cupboard, she thanks her mother and obediently goes to bed. In her room, she cries as it is only when she is alone that she feels it is safe to express her sadness and fear. Mrs. White's projection leaves Carrie emotionally neglected (Chapter 18), angry and feeling powerless to express her anger. She projects her pain onto the mirror and it smashes.

Rita gives the locker room girls one week's detention for bullying Carrie; she wants to punish them more, but the school says one week is enough. Nevertheless, Chris, the ringleader, is furious. Sue, meanwhile, is having feelings of remorse. Rita uses her power and legitimacy as a teacher to give the girls as physically gruelling a detention as she can, and when Chris verbally pushes back, Rita punches her. Rita projects her own unconscious feelings of anger that she was unable to protect Carrie and also her feelings of disgust towards Carrie herself, onto Chris. She uses Chris's obnoxious and elitist demeanour as a hook on which to hang her rage and justify her own inappropriate behaviour whilst in her role as Chris's teacher.

Sue projects her guilt and regret about Carrie onto her boyfriend, Tommy, and asks him to take Carrie to the prom instead of her. In a scene where Sue does homework and Tommy absent-mindedly watches TV, they sit in silence until Tommy reluctantly capitulates saying, '*Ok, I'll do it*,' and only then does Sue smile. Sue's quiet patience is in contrast with the actions of Chris, who gives her boyfriend Billy an unexpected blow job to enlist his assistance in wreaking revenge upon Carrie. Chris projects her rage and disgust towards Carrie onto Billy, calling him an '*idiot*' and a '*dumb shit*.'

Both girls are propelled into the active act of projecting their desires onto their boyfriends by the passive act of not fully engaging with their feelings towards Carrie. They engage with the feeling only enough to know that they do not like the feeling of shame, which has been activated by Rita's perception and punishment of them. They connect more deeply with feelings that seem easier to control. Both girls practice specific attachment behaviours – emotional withdrawal and sexual intimacy – to ensure their boyfriends behave in a manner which can facilitate their projection and give them the outcome they are looking for – a way to manage their own shame.

Despite Sue convincing herself and Tommy that they are doing something nice for Carrie, their projection onto Carrie means that Carrie still remains unseen. When we project onto another, we are obscuring a part of them whilst also obscuring a part of ourselves. Carrie being the subject of Mrs. White and Chris's projections means her environment is dominated by their sense of 'badness.' Being the subject of Sue and Tommy's 'project' and subsequent projections means her environment is dominated by their pity. Carrie struggles to feel like a whole person as the emotional and physical abuse she experiences requires her to bury so many parts of herself in order to survive.

Chris and Sue's Transitions in Projection:

	Sue	Chris
Internal	Shame	Shame
Ego State	Child	Child
Projected	Guilt	Rage
Ego State	Nurturing Parent	Critical Parent
Behaviour	Emotional withdrawal from Tommy	Sexual intimacy with Billy
Desired Outcome	Repair of Carrie. Alleviation of Sue's shame	Destroy Carrie. Alleviation of Chris's shame

The act of projection begins in the internal unconscious and culminates in the external conscious, but often not in our Adult awareness. Unknowingly, by using projections, we increase the internal conflict between the ego states, long term.

For Sue and Chris, we can see how oppositional the behaviour in their process is in contrast to their desired outcome. Often, we bury our uncomfortable feelings in our unconscious to avoid having to deal with them. In this case, the girls are burying their shame. We see how easily both girls are triggered, but instead of understanding their feelings, they seek to turn them into more acceptable feelings that fit within each girl's value system. Rather than sit with her own shame, Sue believes that she is being nice and doing the right thing, as these are important qualities in Sue's identity. Rather than sit with her own shame, Chris believes that exacting revenge is being confident and doing the right thing, as these are important qualities in Chris's identity. When we project, we are reacting to unconscious feelings of discomfort which originate from our Child ego states that, for a multitude of reasons, we choose not to explore and find hard to tolerate.

As I look around the room, I wonder not *if* I have but *who* I have projected onto and what I have projected. I see now how we project onto each other every day in so many ways and how easy it is to do. The week I chose to sit next to one person rather than another, was I, in making this decision, projecting a part of my own inner discomfort? My parents, in their different ways, were not people it was easy to feel emotionally safe with, and as a young girl I struggled, on the inside, to feel secure or confident. Was I more comfortable around men and women who explicitly communicated what they were thinking and feeling, as I projected my own sense of uncertainty and dismissal on others? The coldness I experienced from my mother saddened me, and when I walk towards a person who smiles at me, have I already projected a rejected part of me onto someone else I have walked away from, someone who might have failed to smile?

When Rita discovers Tommy has asked Carrie to the prom, she projects her happy relief onto Carrie, despite her authentic feelings being confusion, worry, fear and anger. Carrie herself is also confused, knowing that Tommy is Sue's boyfriend and she rightly questions Tommy's motives. Tommy insists this is something he wants to do. When Rita demands Sue and Tommy come clean about why Carrie was asked to the prom, Tommy and Sue both react strongly to Rita projecting her fear and worry onto them and insist that they will not be told how to behave, especially since they are trying to do something nice for Carrie. People can often find themselves reacting to unconscious projection. Not knowing exactly why they do not want to do the thing they are being asked to do, but just knowing that it does not feel right for them.

Rita's examination challenges Sue's identity and values and gets her closer to her own shame and Sue resists rather than looking deeper. When Mrs. White tells Carrie she cannot go to the prom, Carrie is insistent that she will go and her mother will not stop her. Carrie is responding to her mother's projection without even being completely sure that going to the prom is the right decision for her.

After agreeing to take part in Chris's revenge plot, Billy kills a pig for its blood. As Billy brings the axe down over and over again, Chris gleefully chants; Chris's projected shame a soundtrack to the pig's death and an ominous foreshadowing of the wider annihilation to come.

Mrs. White notices Carrie hasn't eaten her apple cake and when Carrie says it is because it gives her pimples, Mrs. White declares this is the Lord's way of chastising her. Mrs. White projects her confusion and shame of her own body onto Carrie in relation to sex and the subsequent shame and sadness she feels when her husband leaves her for an intimate relationship with another woman. Carrie says,

> Please see I'm not like you Mama, I'm funny. I mean, all the kids think I'm funny. I don't want to be. I want to be normal. I want to start to try and be a whole person.

Mrs. White responds to Carrie's wish to be 'normal' and her pain of feeling different by throwing a drink in her face. Carrie's seamless continuation of conversation shows how accustomed she has become to her mother's projections and abuse. They have become normalised for Carrie. She has suppressed all her feelings as a protection from her mother's humiliating cruelty and disrespect.

What Carrie chooses to do with her telekinetic abilities is emotionally motivated by the traumatic relationship she has with her mother and the pain of a childhood of misattunement. 'Everything isn't bad, Mama, everything isn't a sin,' pleads Carrie. Mrs. White insists that Carrie's abilities are Satan's work, in the same way as Satan took Carrie's father away. Mrs. White protects herself from the shame and sadness of her husband leaving with a delusional religious fantasy, projecting her pain onto her daughter instead. When Carrie wears her prom dress, Mrs. White says to her daughter, 'I can see your dirty pillows.' Carrie replies, 'Breasts, they're breasts, Mama.'

Chris's revenge comes to life as her friends rig the prom votes for King and Queen, making sure Carrie and Tommy win, and then empty a bucket of pig's blood onto Carrie as she is crowned on stage. Carrie is shocked, humiliated and dripping in blood. Laughter erupts from the crowd as the group project their discomfort onto Carrie by demonically cackling in the face of her embarrassment and making her an object of further ridicule. As Carrie suffers in an echo chamber filled with the horrific sound of their mockery, she starts to remember the words of Tommy and Rita, '*trust me it'll be ok.*' She also remembers the words of her mother prophetically warning that she will be laughed at. Carrie uses her anger and telekinesis to kill everyone in the room.

She kills Chris and Billy on the way home and I remember feeling a sense of relief that in the death of Carrie's ultimate tormentors, there could be some justice for Carrie. I projected my anger onto the villains of this movie in the same way that the horror genre itself allows movie-goers to project their fear, sadness and anger from the tragedies of the world onto the characters on screen, all whilst being contained in the safety of the cinema. A cathartic cinematic release for ourselves from our uncomfortable feelings. When Carrie returns home, Mrs. White has also had a shift in herself and starts talking about Carrie's father.

> *I should have killed myself when he put it in me. After the first time, before we were married, Ralph promised never again. He promised and I believed him – but sin never dies. Sin never dies. At first it was alright we lived sinlessly. We slept in the same bed but we never did it. And then that night I saw him looking down at me that way. We got down on our knees to pray for strength. I smelt the whisky on his breath. And then he took me. He took me. With the stink of filthy roadhouse whisky on his breath. And I liked it. I liked it. With that dirty touching of his hands all over me. I should have given you to God when you were born. But I was weak and backsliding.*

Mrs. White's words read like a confession; a litany of her lifelong projection onto Carrie, and they reek of shame. She stabs Carrie in the back and to protect herself from being killed by her mother, Carrie sends the kitchen knives flying into her mother's hands and body, nailing her mother dead to the door. Mrs. White hangs lifeless like the copious idols of Jesus which decorate the house. Carrie realises what she has done and pulling Mrs. White down to the ground, she holds her mother in her arms, the house catching fire and burning them in it. Despite murdering her mother, Carrie has shown her one loving act after another and modelled how to be a Nurturing Parent for her mother, until the ultimate projection – the shame of Carrie's birth – creates the final annihilation – Carrie's tragic death.

Exercises

1. Have you ever shouted at someone in your life when you were actually feeling angry with yourself or someone else?

2. Think of the emotion you struggle with the most. What is the emotion you feel but don't express?
3. Can you identify an emotional need that you might feel ashamed or embarrassed about and in which ways you may accidentally project these feelings?

Reference

Minuchin, S. (1974). *Families and Family Therapy*. Cambridge, MA: Harvard University Press.

17

Defence Mechanisms and *Heat*

Theory: Defence Mechanisms

The psychological theory that specific behaviours are developed without conscious awareness to psychologically and emotionally keep us safe.

Movie: *Heat (1995)*

A gang of criminals becomes the focus of a relentless LAPD detective in his compulsion to bring them to justice.

What We're Doing?

In this chapter, we will be looking at defence mechanisms (Freud 1894a) and using Michael Mann's movie *Heat* to examine how the characters use these strategies, most of them unconsciously, as part of their choices and behaviour. As we learn about these defence mechanisms, we will start to understand how they relate to the emotional world of our characters. Using my own experience in training, I invite you to consider how defence mechanisms may show up in your life.

My Master's exam was now just weeks away, and it seemed odd, maybe concerning even, that I was feeling so many different, conflicting, emotions. I was excited to reach the end of the training. Four years had flown by and yet at the same time, there were so many moments where it felt like I was stuck, making no progress, standing still. I sensed my feelings were connected to familiar defences, old ways of being in the world that felt almost like old friends, I knew them so well. A strategic way of protecting parts of myself that at a specific moment in my life had not felt brave enough to be exposed to the world, had not felt safe enough to be seen. Despite the original moment having passed, I was using the same defensive strategies I had used then to get about in the world now. Through my training, I had learnt and discovered so much about myself and others but it also felt as if I was on the precipice of arriving somewhere where I knew nothing at all. I wondered if there were spaces, secret gardens if you like, where it was possible not to hold onto the defence mechanisms of the past. A place where it feels like all the defence mechanisms are dismantled and there is nothing left, other than. . .the unknown and the possible.

Definitions of Defence Mechanisms in Response to Stress

Altruism (Comte 1851)
When we engage in acts of service or behaviour seen as 'good,' which allows us to separate from the parts of us that feel 'bad.'

Avoidance (Freud 1894a)
When we have a conscious or unconscious refusal to engage with whatever is able to activate the uncomfortable feeling, whether that be a person, place or situation.

Compensation (Adler 1917)
When we concentrate efforts and energy in one area to balance out other areas where we decide we are less successful.

Denial (Freud 1925)
When we cannot admit to ourselves the existence of a feeling, a situation or event because in doing so we would have to feel uncomfortable feelings so it feels easier to deny the existence of something, deny the truth to ourselves, either consciously or unconsciously.

Disassociation (Janet 1907)
When we mentally and emotionally disconnect ourselves from the pain, shock and reality of a situation.

Displacement (Freud 1900)
When we have a feeling toward one person but redirect that feeling toward someone else who we deem as less threatening.

Intellectualisation (Freud, Anna 1937)
When we use our brains and our cognitive abilities and reasoning to function and put aside the emotional impact of the event and how it affects us.

Passive Aggression (Menninger 1945)
When we indirectly release our anger or frustration in our speech or behaviour.

Projection (Freud 1894a)
When we push onto another person an uncomfortable feeling which we do not want to admit to holding inside ourselves (Chapter 16).

Rationalisation (Freud 1905)
When we attempt to eradicate or minimise an uncomfortable feeling through a logical rationale.

Reaction Formation (Freud 1905)
When we don't feel comfortable accepting a specific emotion we might engage in 'opposite' behaviour in an effort to shift or replace the unwanted feeling.

Regression (Freud 1900)
When we move to a way of behaving more reminiscent of earlier developmental stages of our life.

Repression (Breuer and Freud 1895)
When we unconsciously push down certain feelings and thoughts because feeling them is too overwhelming.

Sublimation (Freud 1905)
When we take the emotion we are feeling and use it to express ourselves in a more acceptable manner.

Suppression (Freud, Anna 1937)
When we consciously push down certain feelings and information, that will lead to those feeling those emotions.

Lieutenant Vincent Hanna cannot take his wife, Justine, to breakfast as she would like him to, as he is rushing to meet his colleague for work. We see Justine adjust her expectations, the SUBLIMATION of her disappointment swallowed in two anxiety pills first thing in the morning to take the edge off her day. She is in DENIAL of how her unmet needs are impacting her emotionally and attempts AVOIDANCE of the more difficult relationship conversations. Vincent's teenage step-daughter Lauren is freaking out about getting ready to go and stay with her biological father and screams at her mother Justine, demanding she, *'pay attention.'* Lauren exhibits DISPLACEMENT, angry at her father but showing anger to her mother instead. Justine holds her daughter close to pacify her but it is clear she is not attuned to the level of Lauren's anxiety and not registering just how much emotional pain her daughter Lauren is in – DENIAL. There is also the AVOIDANCE of the impact that her failed first marriage and an unhappy second marriage is having on her teenage daughter. Justine softens her voice and holds her daughter tightly, too tightly – COMPENSATION.

Neil, the boss of a tight-knit gang of professional criminals, is coordinating the next bank heist. Waingro has been drafted in, new to the team. Slick, one of Neil's men, collects Waingro and en route to the job, he tells Waingro to stop talking. Waingro is visibly offended and we see the instant rage in his eyes. Later, we see Waingro exhibit the same rage when one of the guards, whose head he is holding a gun to, does not respond to his command. Slick tells Waingro that the guard cannot hear him but Waingro is incensed by the guard's refusal to step back and listen to his order. The guard does not move, frozen through fear and submission but Waingro is offended, '*Yeah don't fuck with me.*' Waingro projects his feelings of worthlessness onto the guard and, viewing his life as worth nothing, he kills him – PROJECTION. Neil is furious with Waingro for killing the guard. It is clear to the gang that the guard was not a problem and Waingro had overreacted. Neil feels like Waingro is unreliable, acting in a way that attracts unwanted police attention. In an altercation where Neil roughs him up, Waingro manages to escape.

Vincent and Neil are both driven to be the best detective/criminal they can be, using COMPENSATION and AVOIDANCE in response to difficulties in other areas of their life, like relationships. Vincent uses INTELLECTUALISATION to cope with the tragedies of his work so he does not become overwhelmed with the pain of the victims. Neil says, '*the reward is worth the stretch.*' In reality, this is not true as the level of danger in Neil's bank 'scores' could result in prison for life or even death but he relies on this narrative and uses REPRESSION to cope with his need for intimacy and connection.

Surveying the crime scene at the bank, Vincent becomes aware that he is dealing with consummate professionals. When Vincent returns home late. Justine is upset. Lauren's father did not pick her up as he was supposed to and neither did he call. Lauren has not come out of her bedroom and Justine appears to be annoyed by the fact that she cooked dinner for her and Vincent four hours ago but he also didn't show up – DISPLACEMENT. Justine has made dinner for her detective partner, knowing he regularly works late, and accuses him of withdrawing – PROJECTION. She is already upset she was alone for breakfast and yet knowing he has work, now makes and expects him to show for dinner – SUBLIMATION. Vincent tells Justine that he has three dead bodies that need his attention and struggles to deal with the emotional deficit in his marriage – DENIAL and INTELLECTUALISATION.

Neil meets Eady in a bookstore and she charms him with her openness. He is entirely unpractised in interpersonal relations without experiencing paranoia. As Neil opens up, he tells Eady how his mother died a long time ago and he does not know his father, correctly guessing that Eady, in comparison, is close to her family. Eady's vulnerability continues to dismantle Neil's defences when in response to Neil saying. '*I'm alone. . . I'm not lonely,*' she confesses she is, '*real lonely.*' We learn something more of how Neil maintains his compartmentalised unemotional and cool exterior – SUPPRESSION.

The gang attempt to make even more money by selling their stolen bearer bonds back to their original owner, Roger Van Zant. They do not take into consideration that Van Zant might be outraged that they were stolen in the first place – DENIAL.

Chris, one of the gang, has a fight with his partner Charlene. She says that he's not bringing in enough money from the jobs he's doing, considering the risk he takes. Chris is irritated at himself but lashes out at Charlene for saying what he knows to be true – DISPLACEMENT. He tells her to get out but confides to Neil his fears that Charlene might leave him – REACTION FORMATION. When Neil asks him if he is seeing anyone else, Chris says yes but nothing serious. When Neil asks if Charlene is seeing anyone else, Chris is adamant that Charlene is not – DENIAL. Neil reminds Chris that he cannot have attachments and also live a life of crime. '*Allow nothing to be in your life that you cannot walk out on in 30 seconds flat if you spot the heat around the corner*' – SUPPRESSION and INTELLECTUALISATION. Chris tells Neil he cannot be this way and that Charlene is his whole world.

Don is an ex-offender trying to go legit. He arrives at a diner and introduces himself with conscientious competence as a seasoned grill man to his new boss. The boss does not look at him, speaks in a dismissive tone, issuing a list of menial tasks and forewarns him of the power he holds to send him back to prison. Don is forced to accept this demoralising job and the treatment from his belittling boss as he has limited options – RATIONALISATION, REPRESSION and SUPPRESSION.

Neil calls from an untraceable pay phone and arranges to sell the bonds back to Van Zant. While on the phone, he sees Charlene in a motel with another man, Marciano. Neil orders her to give Chris one last chance at their relationship. Neil's love for Chris makes him angry that his friend might be hurt and he uses his power to threaten and frighten Charlene into doing what he says – PROJECTION. He promises to finance Charlene and their son with a life away from Chris if Chris does not get himself together. He sublimates his aggression with a more acceptable feeling of generosity. Neil's ALTRUISM serves to mask his initial intimidation.

Vincent gets a tip-off about Neil's man Slick and orders surveillance. Neil goes to sell the bonds back to Van Zant but in a bloody shootout, is nearly killed by one of Van Zant's men. The gang go out for dinner and, sitting surrounded by couples, Neil is unable to suppress and disassociate from his loneliness as he usually does. Charlene is trying to act happy despite the fact that it is Neil who has forced her into being there through fear – SUPPRESSION. Neil meets up with Eady again. The gang is unaware that Vincent and his police officers are watching them. The police have rap sheets on Chris and Slick but no information on Neil, '*the loner.*' Vincent finds a dead prostitute bludgeoned to death, one of a series killed by Waingro – DISPLACEMENT and PROJECTION.

Justine and Vincent talk about how she feels excluded. Vincent says he was clear when they met, that she would have to share him with his job but he cannot share the things he sees – '*I gotta hold onto my angst. I preserve it because I need it. It keeps me sharp on the edge*' – RATIONALISATION.

Neil asks Eady to come away with him to New Zealand. To his surprise, he finds himself building an attachment to Eady while recommending that Chris limit his own – DENIAL. Neil and Chris are on the next job when one of Vincent's men falls in the surveillance truck and makes a noise. Neil gets spooked and tells Chris they must leave. Vincent is raging and calls off the operation, fearing that the most they will be able to charge the gang with is a lesser misdemeanour charge. Angry with the situation, he orders everyone to fall back, '*I have tactical command that supersedes your rank*,' throwing his walkie-talkie at the wall – PROJECTION. Neil is now aware that the LAPD is monitoring the gang's every move, and that their next score will be doubly dangerous. Vincent is open about his broken attachments and his obsession with his job whilst Justine emotionally withdraws. She is sad and angry and expresses both by being deliberately provocative and dressing up for a date with another man whilst giving Vincent the silent treatment – PASSIVE AGGRESSION. Vincent chases Neil down the highway but instead of arresting him, he suggests they share a cup of coffee. Here we see the intimacy lacking in both their lives. Neil asks Vincent how he expects to have successful relationships, chasing guys like him who specifically do not form attachments so they can evade the law. Vincent tells Neil about his recurring dream of all the victims he has ever encountered who just look at him with black eyeballs from their head wounds and decomposing, offensive-smelling bodies. Neil tells Vincent of a dream where he is drowning and he must somehow come out of the dream to breathe or he'll die. He says it's about not having enough time to do the things he wants to do. The intimate way the men share their dreams with each other reveals unconscious processes where they have entered into early states of feeling – REGRESSION. Drowning in dreams symbolises both the stress of living and the existential fear of being alive.

Van Zant is terrified, unable to sleep since being threatened by Neil and is living unshaven in his office. Waingro offers to help him find Neil for a fee. The police find Marciano and entrap him to get to Charlene, and eventually Chris. Neil asks Don to be their driver on the next job. Don has tried his best to live a legitimate life but the hardship and disrespect prove too much and he agrees. The gang go into the bank, but a dramatic shootout between the police and the gang ensures, bullets flying everywhere. Don dies as do numerous police officers, including some from Vincent's team. Vincent shoots Slick dead and Chris is wounded. Neil carries Chris, critically injured, on his back, discovering that it is Waingro who has sold him out to the police. Neil kills Van Zant – PROJECTION. Vincent tracks Neil, knowing he will be wanting to kill Waingro next.

The police try to use Charlene as bait to lure her boyfriend, Chris. She pushes down her sadness to save Chris – SUPPRESSION. She lies to the police that it is not Chris in the car that has just pulled up. She is conflicted but would rather let him go than entrap him with the police. She surreptitiously communicates to Chris that he should turn around and go back as the police are with her.

Vincent finds Lauren in a bath of her own blood after an attempted suicide – SUBLIMATION. Justine asks Vincent if there is hope for them. Vincent says, '*all I am is what I am going after,*' – DISASSOCIATION. Neil kills Waingro – PROJECTION. He is about to reunite with Eady when he sees Vincent and knows he must make a choice. Neil walks away from Eady – SUPPRESSION and INTELLECTUALISATION. Vincent and Neil try to evade each other but Vincent fatally shoots Neil – PROJECTION. Neil holds his hand out and Vincent takes it so that he does not die alone.

I realised that, like Neil, my chosen seat in classrooms, restaurants and other public spaces are located near the exit allowing me to be gone in thirty seconds if I feel the heat. I also realised I was using defence mechanisms of rationalisation and suppression to distance myself from my fear. I was terrified to take my exam. I was scared of being seen in the exam but also wanted to be seen and to have the opportunity to demonstrate everything I had learnt and show what I knew. The fear of what could happen in the exam had me go straight to my core belief – my Don't Succeed (Chapter 15), that I am not good enough. The shame of not being good enough and the loss of an ability to succeed as a young girl at school had me stuck. Oscillating between spaces of fear and loss, I projected onto the examiners that they would be unpropitious until Pagan said, '*remember the examiners are all rooting for you – they want you to pass.*' I remember being blown away by this concept! Really? Truly? They want the best for me? The way we see the world, ourselves and each other directly influences our use of defence mechanisms.

Exercises

1. When are occasions that, like Vincent, you hold on to your angst/anger because you believe you need it?
2. Are there times that, like Neil, you hold back from committing to attachments/relationships and could leave them and walk away, emotionally or physically, in 30 seconds if you needed to?
3. Vincent says, '*All I am is what I am going after.*' What do you really want in life and how does how you live your life contradict that?

References

Adler, A. (1917). *Study of Organ Inferiority and Its Psychical Compensation: A Contribution to Clinical Medicine* (trans. J.E. Coffey). New York: Nervous and Mental Disease Publishing Co.

Breuer, J. and Freud, S. (1895). *Studies on Hysteria* (trans. James and A. Strachey). London: Penguin.

Comte, A. (1851). *System of Positive Polity* (trans. J.H. Bridges). London: Longmans, Green and Co.

Freud, S. (1894a). The neuro-psychoses of defence. *Neurologisches Centralblatt* 13: 4–11; 36–43.

Freud, S. (1894b). The neuro-psychoses of defence. In: *The Standard Edition of the Complete Psychological Works of Sigmund Freud, Vol. III (1893–1899): Early Psycho-Analytic Publications* (ed. J. Strachey), 41–61. London: Hogarth Press and the Institute of Psycho-Analysis.

Freud, S. (1900). The interpretation of dreams. In: *The Standard Edition of the Complete Psychological Works of Sigmund Freud, Vol. IV–V (1900–1901)* (trans. J. Strachey) (ed. J. Strachey). London: Hogarth Press and the Institute of Psycho-Analysis.

Freud, S. (1905). Three essays on the theory of sexuality. In: *The Standard Edition of the Complete Psychological Works of Sigmund Freud, Vol. VII (1901–1905)* (trans. J. Strachey) (ed. J. Strachey). London: Hogarth Press and the Institute of Psycho-Analysis.

Freud, S. (1925). Negotion. In: *The Standard Edition of the Complete Psychological Works of Sigmund Freud, Vol. XIX (1923–1925): The Ego and the Id and Other Works* (trans. J. Strachey) (ed. J. Strachey), 235–239. London: Hogarth Press and the Institute of Psycho-Analysis.

Freud, A. (1937). *The Ego and the Mechanisms of Defence* (trans. C. Baines). London: Hogarth Press and the Institute of Psycho-Analysis.

Janet, P. (1907). *The Major Symptoms of Hysteria: Fifteen Lectures Given in the Medical School of Harvard University*. New York: Macmillan.

Menninger, W.C. (1945). A psychiatric evaluation of military service. US War Department, Technical Bulletin.

18

Childhood Emotional Neglect and *Another Happy Day*

Theory: Childhood Emotional Neglect

The experience of repeated emotional misattunements during childhood resulting in complex internal and relational neurosis in adulthood.

Movie: *Another Happy Day (2011)*

Lyn attends a family wedding that explosively brings together remarried parents, an aggrieved spouse, and hurt adult children. We see painful childhood triggers resurface with her mother Doris.

What We're Doing?

In this chapter, we will be looking at the psychological theory of Childhood Emotional Neglect in the movie, *Another Happy Day*. As we learn about the theory, we will use it to understand and explore how the characters in the movie struggle in their lives and why. Using my own experience in training, I invite you to consider how the theory may relate to your life.

Growing up, I always spoke too much. '*You always want to talk about something,*' my mother would say. Her comment was less of a complimentary observation and more of a verbalised irritation. And she wasn't wrong. I did want to talk. About everything. Things I felt, things I did not feel, things I loved and things I hated. And even more specifically, I wanted to talk to her about the two of us. I couldn't think of anything nicer than my mother knowing about and sharing my emotional world. But this wasn't a place, I see now, that my mother wanted to go, despite my repeated invitations. For her, it was tiring, shaming and frightening. Over the four years of training, I had shared so much of my emotional world with a group of strangers that it seemed incredible they knew more about me than my own mother did.

In *Another Happy Day*, we meet Lyn, a mercurial mother of four. Dylan (late 20s) and Alice (early 20s) are from her previous marriage to Paul. Eliot (16 years old) and Ben (11 years old) are from her current marriage to Lee. Lyn carries the weight of her acrimonious relationship with Paul, who she will encounter in a few hours. Lyn has a difficult relationship with Paul's new wife Patty, who raised and is stepmother to Dylan whose wedding they are all about to attend.

Lyn is about to exit a petrol station when Eliot makes a sardonic reference to his mother having engaged in a sexual encounter in the toilet as a way to ease the tensions of the upcoming family reunion. Eliot is reacting to the awkwardness and tension that Lyn emanates but is trying to ignore. '*Shut up and get in the car Eliot*,' she retorts. In the car on the drive to Lyn's parents' house, where they are staying, Eliot probes his mother to answer questions on the specifics of their estranged family relationships while capturing footage for a video he and Ben are making. Lyn is trying to be patient and, in spite of herself, laughs at Eliot's humour. But when his questioning starts triggering her and gets too close to the bone, she loses focus while driving and only narrowly avoids a collision, screaming at the boys, '*Turn that fucking camera off.*' When we experience stress over a prolonged period, it can dysregulate the body's natural responses; Lyn often finds herself in either fight or flight.

Lyn says to her sons, '*Please, I'm begging you, don't make this any more difficult for me than this already is.*' Though Lyn is being honest, her emotionally demanding language asks her children to look after her rather than the other way around, a sign of Parentification (Chapter 8). '*The last time you went to rehab I told them you were in Sweden*,' Lyn tells Eliot as they arrive. Eliot is shocked and becomes flustered that he does not know enough about Sweden to maintain the lie, whilst internalising the message that the part of him that is suffering must stay shamefully hidden.

At her parents' house, we meet Lyn's sisters, Bonnie and Donna, who cackle like witches while making jokes at Eliot's expense. He squirms and physically retreats into his body. The sisters also make jokes about their father, at which Lyn laughs more easily. The joking continues: the aunts and uncles about their nephew, and the cousins about their aunt. The family baton to laugh at people rather than with them is passed around and the jokes are funny until they land on the individual concerned. Here, the hurt is left to fester unaddressed.

BONNIE:	*Don't get all worked up, Lyn.*
DORIS:	*Can we please not get into a whole thing.*
BOTH GIRLS:	*I'm not getting into a whole thing.*
HUSBAND:	*Ladies, can't we just get along?*

Conversations about other topics are also curtailed, swept under the proverbial carpet and diminished in importance. '*Who goes to a therapist to talk to their ex-husband?*' says Bonnie, in disgust, about Lyn. Certain conversations feel hard to have in the family but when help is sought from outside the family on how to communicate better, the need for this help is minimised and dismissed.

Lyn is struggling with Eliot's personality and behaviour. She has been asked questions by Eliot's doctor about his family history regarding emotional struggles and goes to ask her mother, Doris.

DORIS: *I don't know why you ask me these kinds of questions.*
LYN: *So nobody in your family had any history of depression, obsessive compulsive disorder or severe. . .?*
DORIS: *No.*
LYN: *Ok, so where'd he come from, Mum?*

Eliot's way of being in the world is so troubling for Lyn that she cannot see the similarities in their pain and that Eliot's childhood might have impacted him in ways which leave him feeling disconnected from the world.

LYN: *Didn't Dad's Dad have some kind of. . .didn't he drink heavily?*
DORIS: *Yeah, but that was uh. . .*
LYN: *Did he die of drinking?!*
DORIS: *No, of course not!* (Pause) *He shot himself.*
LYN: *I'd say that's something!*
DORIS: *It was a different time, Lyn. It was during the depression. A lot of people shot themselves.*

Through Lyn and her mother's conversations, we see the impact of generational trauma. The cultural tragedies specific to an era, e.g. suicide during an economic depression, have been normalised as part of a necessary acceptance of reality. The need to normalise has continued through the family lineage. Being an alcoholic carries a stigma, while taking your own life is part of life. Childhood Emotional Neglect is a symptom of generational trauma and is characterised by its invisibility through normalising what is not okay. Not having a parent at all is a huge and unequalled loss for a child but having any kind of parent also brings complex challenges. Emotional neglect of a child can lead to cumulative trauma and subsequent emotional issues in adulthood.

Lyn is concerned about the imminent arrival of Alice, who has been struggling emotionally for a long time. Alice has a history of self-harming and is concerned about the likelihood of certain conversations occurring with her father, who she has had little to do with for many years. Lyn wants to convince Paul that talking is not best for Alice as she is emotionally fragile. Despite a mother wanting to protect her child, the familiar act of avoiding communication continues and has been passed down from Lyn's mother to

Lyn. It appears to have stopped with Eliot, who is uncomfortable lying and who is seen as obnoxious because he says the things that no one else is saying but everyone is thinking. Often, there is one person in a family who is unconsciously tasked with being the family mouthpiece. This role can lead to scapegoating, which is also a symptom of Childhood Emotional Neglect.

In the run-up to the wedding, Eliot regularly upsets those around him. *'Is it my genes? Am I a bad mother?'* Lyn asks Ben, who has been diagnosed with mild Asperger's syndrome. He answers maturely and methodically that he has been thinking about this very same thing. He says that, looking at the four children and their individual struggles, he has come to the conclusion that Lyn must be a bad mother, as she is the common denominator between them all. Ben asks Eliot if he is going to beat up Paul because Paul used to physically abuse Lyn when they were married. Eliot answers that he himself has hit Lyn before. Again, we see how the cycles of abuse and trauma pass through generations and how negative legacies which originate from childhood are also neglected.

Eliot steals fentanyl from his grandfather's drawer to get high and passes out on the bathroom floor. Eliot has learnt to push his feelings down and attempts to sublimate the disconcerting sense of isolation where it feels like there is no one who understands him. He loses himself in the haze of fentanyl to disassociate his body and mind, splitting himself off from his own emotional awareness, preferring emotional numbness to emotional overwhelm or even just the feeling of sadness.

In 1995 the Centres for Disease Control and Prevention (CDC) began the Adverse Childhood Experiences (ACEs) study (Sawyer et al. 2024) in which a group of 10 adverse childhood situations were identified as increasing the risk of these children suffering negative health and social outcomes over the course of their life and into adulthood including being at higher risk for depression, anxiety, diabetes, heart disease, autoimmune diseases and impaired memory.

 1. Physical Abuse
 2. Sexual Abuse
 3. Emotional Abuse
 4. Physical Neglect
 5. Emotional Neglect
 6. Mental Illness
 7. Family member in prison
 8. Violence towards the mother
 9. Substance Abuse
10. Divorce

It is interesting to note that the ACEs criteria recognises violence towards the mother, an undoubtedly 'adverse' childhood experience, but *Another Happy Day* explores the impact that physical or emotional abuse perpetrated against the child's mother by her own parents can have on the child. So often the abuser has at some point also been the abused. Lyn's pain and her ability to tolerate physical abuse from Paul and Eliot began with Doris emotionally abusing Lyn. Doris' way of coping with her unhappiness was to project her shame and anger onto her daughter. Divorce makes the list not because of any of its moral or philosophical ramifications but because of the unprocessed trauma it often results in. Unprocessed trauma is emotion that is held in the body and not felt and released. Divorce involves the loss of dreams and ideals. When Lyn and Paul married, they had expectations and for Lyn, being physically abused was not one of them. Paul, unhappy in his marriage, projected his anger onto Lyn by beating her. Their collective unprocessed trauma impacts Alice, who copes with her unprocessed trauma by self-harming.

Doris is upset about her husband. All his life, he has liked his pancakes golden and fluffy and now she says he wants them as *'black as the lady on the syrup bottle.'* She asks Ben not to tell anyone what she said, aware that there are those in the family that might take offence to this comment. Ben says his grandmother is twice as old as the civil rights movement anyway. His maths is a loving attempt to excuse his grandmother from her problematic rhetoric. Yet if we are acknowledging that the history of racism has evolved over time, we must also acknowledge that a style of parenting where the child is emotionally neglected is also outdated.

Paul demanded that if Lyn left the marriage, he would only allow her to take Alice but not both children. He also said that if she tried to take both children, he would block her from taking any of them. Violence towards the mother can be physical as well as emotional. We see Eliot call his Mum *'a fucking bitch,'* echoing the attitude of Paul, when she refuses to let him go out. He also spits in her face and physically intimidates her as he pushes her to the floor.

Lyn's father, Joe, asks, *'what's wrong with Eliot? He's got a good life.'* Lyn explains to him that Eliot suffers with depression, obsessive-compulsive disorder, severe anxiety, Tourette's syndrome and difficulty managing his emotions. Her father seems not to hear. *'He goes to the best schools, he's a good-looking kid.'* Childhood Emotional Neglect is often missed because, as with Eliot, external factors can appear to compensate for the sadness and emptiness felt on the inside. The inability to recognise and manage different emotions and moderate behaviour in educational settings can be signs of childhood emotional neglect. Joe cannot pinpoint a single, traumatic event in Eliot's life, the opposite in fact. His assumption that Eliot has no issues ignores, and thus compounds, the difficult and often hard-to-identify feelings of emotional neglect.

Lyn asks Eliot where all these feelings come from. *'From the moment I get here I'm forced to lie, lie about being in fucking Sweden and trying to hide the fact that I have fucking issues. You can't escape,'* answers Eliot. And we see that taking fentanyl was an attempt to do exactly that, to escape the pain. *'You drive yourself crazy and Alice cuts herself.'*

Lyn's questioning of Eliot does many things. She attunes to Eliot by acknowledging his feelings. She shows respect for his internal process and learns something about herself as well. She shows curiosity and interest in who he is and what it is like to be Eliot in this world – how he might respond as a child to the decisions his parents make. There is an emotional security she offers Eliot; that despite how badly he has behaved, his behaviour is not all he is and she is able to attach to another part of him. Lyn is not condoning his behaviour but she is accepting that there is a part of Eliot in pain. This acceptance makes Eliot feel valued and allows him to feel his mother can see him exactly as he is. Lyn's entire demeanour expresses her love and compassion toward Eliot and she models caring adult behaviour that Eliot will be able to offer to himself one day.

After Lyn sews sleeves onto Alice's bridesmaid dress so that she does not have to feel self-conscious about the cuts on her arms, Doris says, '*All I'm saying is that I think Alice would like to fit in with the rest of the party rather than sticking out like a sore thumb.*' Lyn's mother does not want to accept that Paul was abusive to Lyn or that her granddaughter Alice has had an emotional reaction to her parents' abusive marriage – she chooses to focus on the sleeves as the problem rather than the emotional turmoil of her daughter's marriage and its repercussions on the next generation. When a child's emotions are neglected, they find other ways to manifest.

Lyn explains in a family therapy session that Alice was trying to convert her emotional pain into something tangible – physical pain. Lyn tries to communicate to her whole family that everything in Alice's life has been beyond her control and that Alice's self harming is a way of trying to gain some control after her parents' divorce, when she was forced to spend summers with Paul and grow up without her brother. In response to Lyn's explanation of Alice having no control, Doris spits, '*But you did.*' The shock on Lyn's face as her mother voices her fierce disapproval in front of Paul and Patty is tragically palpable. Lyn pleads with Paul to confirm, in front of her parents, whether her hazy memory is correct and he did punch her in the face whilst Alice, as a terrified toddler, clung to her skirt. Paul confirms that he did indeed assault her. Lyn looks at her mother repeatedly, who refuses to make eye contact. Her father reassuringly puts a hand on Paul's shoulder and says, '*it must feel good to get that off your chest, Son.*' The comments made by her parents in family therapy illustrate that indifference and insensitivity inflicted on a child can continue long into adulthood.

LYN: *Why weren't you on my side? You're my mother.*

The scene epitomises the unbearable wounding of emotional neglect that Lyn has endured and still endures. What the movie does so effortlessly is canonise the everyday casual remarks that family members say to one another and how these hurtful projections can cause such deep lacerations. Lyn walks out into the expanse of the garden in an attempt to get away from the pain she feels being repeatedly missed by her parents. She falls down into the grass and cries. Eliot walks over to his collapsed mother and sits down beside her. Lyn shuffles her fetal-shaped body nearer her son and lays her head in his lap, sobbing. Eliot is able to offer Lyn his love, his physical body and his time because Lyn had modelled this same compassion for him earlier.

Lyn asks her mother *'Why is it you have never learned to just keep quiet? Never had the decency or the respect or the consideration to keep anything private.'* It is almost as if, despite hearing about her daughter's abusive marriage and having it confirmed by her ex-son-in-law, she is angry that it is being talked about out in the open and she would rather Lyn had kept such details to herself. Lyn's pain has somehow offended Doris with its messy, unkempt nature. They are at the kitchen table late at night Lyn's mother is uncharacteristically emotional. She is upset about her husband's ill-health, about how she could soon become a widow and the silence she will face. She is crying and suddenly reveals her emotions rather than suppressing them. Then, all at once, as if catching herself, exposed, she adopts a passive-aggressive tone, and says, *'You got me – that's what you came down here for, isn't it?'* Doris is terrified of her own emotions and catching herself expressing them, she turns her terror into rage and projects this onto Lyn. This scene demonstrates how there is no emotional space for Lyn in her relationship with her vulnerable, narcissistic mother. Lyn's need and desire to connect to Doris is shamed. Doris projects her own shame and uncomfortable feelings onto Lyn as if Lyn's main objective was to cause her mother pain. Wanting to connect is a biological human need and when those needs are neglected, the felt stress can lead to an inability to feel joy. Adults suffering from Childhood Emotional Neglect often report feelings of chronic emptiness born from a lack of attunement and consistent chipping away at their self-worth (Erskine et al. 1999).

By the time the wedding arrives, Alice has been forced to have conversations and find the words she did not want to speak. She has felt feelings she did not want to feel. She has cried tears she did not want to cry. Despite her mother trying to protect her, Alice, now an adult, found herself needing to find her own nurturing mother/Adult ego state and protect herself. Finally, she is able to calmly, confidently and without damaging herself, say *'no'* to her father. This is what Alice must do for herself and for her healing. It is not easy for Alice and it is not what she ideally wanted but sometimes, even in families where there is a strong cultural and societal expectation to stay together, peace, growth and happiness come from allowing a dysfunctional dynamic to break. This allows the toxic cycle to end and something new to begin for everyone.

Trauma can include substantial developmental and vicarious trauma, even in the absence of a single traumatic episode or experience, like in the case of Childhood Emotional Neglect. This pain accumulates over years, impacting core beliefs and a person's expectations and assumptions of the world. Emotional neglect fosters a hidden and insidious sense of shame, '*I am not good enough.*' Addiction is a way of numbing a person's relational needs and children of parents currently suffering with addictions or who have suffered with addictions in the past will often be told, '*You're so needy*' when they demand something that the adult is unable to give. The shame of how it feels to be asked is hard to tolerate, and so the trauma carries on.

So many scenes in this movie reminded me of my mother and I felt the shame and blame that filled the spaces where, at different times, my whole family wanted to be seen, to be heard and to feel loved. I knew I had to be a nurturing mother to myself, but what was I supposed to do with the grief and the loss of the relationship I wanted? A child first sees themselves through the eyes of their mother/caregiver. How could I be recognised as the person I truly was when viewed through the distorted lens of a woman who was herself the product of generational trauma? Though it might be that the mother plays a pivotal role in the child's emotional neglect, this mother will often have also been emotionally neglected herself, and may not have even known it. What did I know about my mother's own child-hood? Or her mother, and her childhood? And so it goes on.

The shame and loss in Childhood Emotional Neglect is profound and the person sitting next to you on the train may be deeply suffering, but on the outside, it is hard to tell. This is the legacy of generational trauma, it keeps being passed on until someone – Lyn, Eliot, Alice, me, you – breaks the cycle.

Exercises

1. Do you experience feelings of emptiness or find it hard to derive joy from your life or the things you achieve? Write about this feeling of emptiness. How long do you remember it being there? When are you aware of it the most? Are there times you try to hide your emptiness?
2. Does it feel as if it's always about the next thing/goal? Are there moments in your life you wish you could have enjoyed more?
3. What do you remember about your parents' relationship to joy in childhood? Do you remember them finding joy in you?

References

Erskine, R., Moursund, J., Trautmann, R. et al. (1999). *Beyond Empathy*. Philadelphia: Brunner/Mazel.

Sawyer, K., Kempe, S., Carwana, M. et al. (2024). Global and inclusive considera-tions for the future of ACEs research. *Child Protection and Practice*. 3: 100054.

19

Shame and *American History X*

Theory: Shame

The psychological theory of shame: the affect and internal emotion of not feeling good enough.

Movie: *American History X (1998)*

A young White man becomes influenced by a White supremacist group leader after his father dies, but after being going sent to prison for brutally killing a Black man, he gets out and starts to question his values and the world he has been living in versus the less hateful world which he would like to live in.

What We're Doing?

In this chapter, we will be looking at the psychological theory of shame in the movie *American History X*. As we learn about shame and the different ways in which the characters respond to shame, we will use it to understand and explore the events that unfold. Using my own experience in training, I invite you to consider how the theory may relate to your life.

It was a hot day in summer, burning leather seats in the family Ford estate and me in my teens. My father goes into a Sri Lankan food store to buy some samosas whilst I sit in the car waiting for him, as I had been told to do. I had initially said I did not want any samosas, but now I was watching through the glass as he chatted to the shop owner and imagined the taste of the delicious meat-filled pastry triangles. Knowing I must act quickly, I bound out of the car and almost fall into the shop. The shop owner, finding my urgency amusing, smiles and asked if I am hungry. I start talking about how tasty I had dreamt these samosas would be and that yes, thinking about them had made me hungry. We paid for the now larger order of samosas and my father and I headed back to the car. The door shut, my father turned to me, disgust all over his face, '*Never do that again,*' he said angrily. This was not the same voice he had used with the shop owner and the dichotomy scared me. '*Don't ever be so familiar in public.*'

It would be years before I was able to give a name to the sensations and feelings I experienced in that moment. Shame is a notoriously slippery state to locate and to identify. Shame is not a word that was ever mentioned in my family despite it being everpresent. At the time, I was unaware that the flushed burning in my torso and face was the effect of shame, nor was I aware of the way I lowered my head and eyes as he admonished me or the way my body sank into itself. My positive and joyful samosa experience had been interrupted. I was confused. I had behaved badly, shamefully, but I did not really understand what I had done.

Decades later, a tutor expresses her surprise that I am sitting my psychotherapy Master's exam sooner than she would expect. I am confused; a prominent feature of the course was the fact that students were encouraged to progress at their own pace. I explain that I am ready – the results of my diploma were excellent and I received a distinction in my dissertation. The main point she seemed to be making was that it was not something that other people did or had done before, with the exception of one esteemed lecturer. This time, I recognised the sensations and knew all too well the feelings of shame that flowed through me. The comparison to others made me feel like I was getting it wrong, not doing it right, not good enough. Though I knew I did not want to be compared to anyone, that is exactly what she was doing. I wanted to break free from my own personal limitations, to exceed my own self-imposed constraints on what I was able to achieve. I felt shame for wanting, for wanting something different to what others wanted for me.

American History X unfolds in carefully edited flashbacks shot in black and white. Two family dinners take place. The first sees our main character, Derek (age 18), with his mother Doris and her Jewish boyfriend Murray, Derek's brother Danny, their sister Davina and Derek's girlfriend Stacy. Derek, seated at the head of the table, is having a heated debate using racist terminology to refer to Black people, during which Murray comments that the recent city riots are '*an irrational act, an expression of rage by people who feel neglected and turned away by the system.*' This leads to an exchange of different opinions over the Rodney King case and Derek uses his brother, Danny, to explain how different the conversation would have been if the police were being asked to respond to an incident involving someone they loved. The poignancy and symmetry of this example is later echoed in the film's climactic ending when Danny is shot dead in a school shooting, retaliation brought about by his assuming a White supremacist gang identity, an idealised identity he had inherited from Derek.

Despite the skewed racist rhetoric, the conversation only escalates at the point where Davina refuses to listen to Stacey's far-right views and tries to leave the table. Derek becomes instantly enraged. '*Sit down, shut your mouth and give my girlfriend some respect!*' he says. Derek stands up using his body to block Davina's path and physically intimidates his sister so she cannot move. He grabs Davina by the hair and, seemingly crazed, pulls her backwards, ramming fistfuls of cake into her mouth while his sister struggles to breathe. Doris and Murray are shouting and pleading for Derek to stop. Danny is slumped on the floor holding his head in his hand. '*You need to learn some manners, Davina!*' The family dinner has turned savage.

Derek responds to his internal rage by humiliating others. He funnels his rage into something active, something he can control through his humiliation of Davina. Derek then attacks Murray stressing that this is his family and he will never allow some '*kike to fuck my mother*.' Derek is able to become enraged listening to Murray's leftist politics and by the fact that he is Jewish, but when he speaks to his mother, we hear something else come through. '*You disgust me. How could you bring him to my father's table? Your hair and that dress. . .all tarted up.*'

Derek's speech reveals that in assuming his role as head of the house, he has also laid claim to his mother's sexual boundaries. It is an angry little boy speaking when Derek asks '*what has happened to my family, where is my father?*' He demands Davina give Stacy respect, while he gives his own mother none – the markers don't tally. Derek's grief in losing his father, Dennis – three years ago, has not been processed. Derek is unable to allow himself the vulnerability to express his loss. The state of grief often includes the shame of not being able to control the events around us or our response to them. Since his father passed, Derek has established himself as a fearless neo-Nazi leader, turning his shame into humiliating fury as a way to wall himself off from a potent sense of powerlessness. In this way, he is able to keep his father's memory alive and keep his family the way he remembers, but most of all he is able to manage his inner emotional turmoil.

Doris stands up to Derek, telling him she is '*ashamed you came out of my body!*' She tells him to leave and that this is his last night in her house. Just hours later, Danny interrupts Derek and Stacy having sex to tell Derek that a couple of guys are trying to steal Derek's car. Naked, Stacy is embarrassed and her shame of sex is directorially juxtaposed with the family's shame of Derek's next moments. He shoots one of the men, drags his body to the pavement at gunpoint and forces him to open his mouth, teeth on the curb. Then he stomps on the man's head with his boot, killing him. Danny screams for him to stop – but Derek does not. Derek serves three years for the voluntary manslaughter of the Black would-be thief.

Danny's voiceover highlights that this is a movie about what we do or don't do with our own shame, such as when he says that their family problems started long before their father was murdered. But that they did start with their father. This is shown through the second family dinner scene, a flashback to when Derek's father was still alive. Derek is inspired by a Black history teacher, Mr. Sweeney, '*this guy's unbelievable, I've never had a teacher like this, he's got like two PhDs, I don't know what he's doing teaching at our school.*' Sweeney is having his pupils read different books from the ones on the curriculum, specifically '*Native Son*,' a story by Richard Wright. The obvious social injustice is paralleled in the contrast of Derek's voluntary manslaughter charge for the intentional killing of a Black man, and the sentencing to death of a Black man for the accidental killing of a White woman in Wright's book. Dennis does not know the book, but we sense his discomfort at Derek's comment that Mr. Sweeney is too well educated to be teaching at his school. Doris makes a joke about the school not teaching the kinds of books her husband reads. Dennis explains to Derek that he needs to question what this means and asks if they are going to get rid of great books by White authors to make space for books written by Black authors. Dennis does not educate his son on why books by Black authors are only just starting to be taught in schools or explore why he himself might struggle to understand that books written by non-White authors can also be great books. Dennis does, however, share with his son that a White colleague at work has been passed over by a Black colleague who is not as competent, but that the move ticked the box of 'affirmative action,' leaving Derek with someone who is less able but yet needs to be '*watching my back, responsible for my life.*'

Dennis does not model for Derek any of his shame but only his indignation. Without offering the historical context of slavery, violence and inhumane, racially motivated subjugation, he talks of a '*hidden agenda*', warning of '*nigger bullshit.*' Dennis covers his shame with rage. When Danny says, '*it's hard to look back and see the truth about the people you love,*' he is talking about his shame-filled father and how Derek, the brother Danny put on a pedestal, went on to internalise and then later externalise his father's shame, an identity Danny would assimilate and which would eventually lead to his own death as a teenager.

American History X is a film about race but long before discussions on race existed, there was and still is, shame. Psychologist Silvan Tomkins (1991) explored shame as one of the biological processes human beings are born with and one that is innately used to respond to situations where a process of joy is interrupted. This is interesting because there is a perception that shame is often synonymous with wrongful behaviour. Tomkins posits that there is not always a wrong despite us often seeing blame as a way to correct a wrong when shame is experienced. He explains that the effect of shame is the first notion of a fluctuation in feeling, an interruption in the state of joy or neutrality that went before it. This feeling is then moulded and shaped, like clay being fired and hardened, in a kiln of inter-generational and generational experiences and stories.

That said, there are plenty of wrong behaviours in the lives of the characters in *American History X*. Humiliation is seen to be triggered when shame is experienced. Dennis is concerned that the Black firefighter will not be able to protect him. When Dennis dies attending to a fire in a suspected drug den, Derek believes that his father's fear has been confirmed. He takes the story he heard from his father and it becomes the nexus of Derek's experiences, preventing him from processing any of the hurt and pain of losing his father. Instead of feeling the shame of his grief, Derek only engages with the anger; humiliating Davina and dismissing her liberal opinions, humiliating his mother who wishes to find love again, humiliating Murray for being Jewish and humiliating and killing the man who tried to steal the car his father left him.

In prison, Derek attaches himself to a White supremacist group for protection, to prevent retaliation by a Black gang in response to the crime Derek has committed. Though Derek's group has the Nazi symbol tattooed on their bodies, it is clear that life in prison requires more flexibility when it comes to making friends and surviving. Derek gets a job working the laundry with a Black inmate, Lamont. Over the course of Derek's sentence, we see Lamont patiently persist in cultivating a friendship with Derek. Derek holds out on forging a respectful relationship with a Black man for as long as he possibly can, but Lamont's civility and joviality are too strong for Derek to ignore despite his best intentions.

Derek is incensed when he notices one of his crew buying drugs from the Mexicans. He responds with a rigidity and righteousness to which the White neo-Nazi gang takes offence. They cover their shame with an attack on Derek; shown in a brutal gang rape scene in the prison shower. The shame that Derek carries can be physically seen in the way he walks, his legs forced apart by the pain of his injuries. He no longer has the protection of a crew and sits alone with his head down and eyes averted – common physical signs of shame. His shame is most visible as he breaks down and cries when his old teacher, Mr. Sweeney, comes to visit him.

There is shame for Derek in knowing that the values of the White supremacist philosophy to which he has attached himself were not enough to save him from being sexually assaulted by his own people. This idea mirrors the first dinner scene conversation where Derek points out the immorality of Black people robbing from their own and Murray responds by reminding Derek that White people are also capable of hurting their own. Derek feels the shame of seeing the truth in Murray's words after his White friends have raped him and left him to bleed out on the shower room floor. He feels the shame that it is his Black teacher, Mr. Sweeney who sits beside him and comforts him and the fact that it is his Black friend, Lamont, who persuades the other Black inmates not to seek their revenge despite Derek being defenceless and open to attack. He is then left with the shame of remaining attached to a racist ideology; the shame of choosing a path because of a perceived sense of loyalty to his father and the shame of loss. Here begins Derek's journey of self-reflection.

Nathanson (1992) continued Tomkins's work with his 'Compass of Shame' (Fig. 19.1). He offers four behaviours the shamed individual will employ instead of experiencing their own shame: withdrawal, avoidance, attack on the other and/or attack of the self.

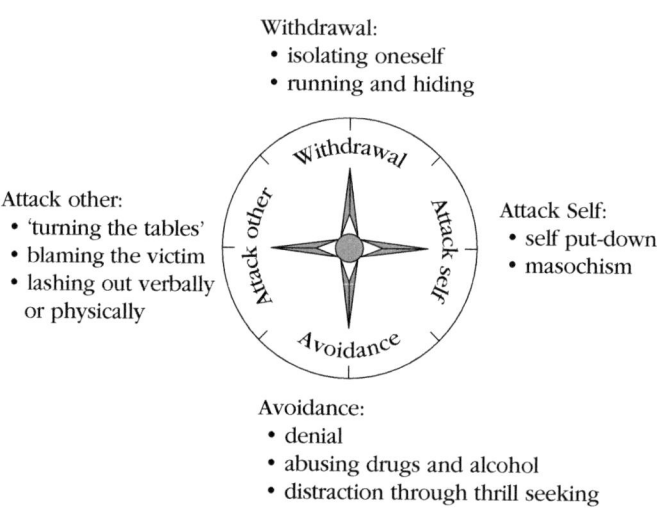

Fig. 19.1   Compass of Shame – Donald Nathanson

Derek uses 'attack other' when he kills. He uses 'avoidance' by attaching himself to the supremacist ideology to avoid processing the grief of his father's death. He uses 'withdrawal' in prison after he is attacked.

When Derek gets out of prison and returns home, he is a different person. He enters the family home with different ideas and wants a different life for himself, his family and his brother Danny, who has already been partly lured in by the same charismatic group leader that seduced Derek. The film ends with the poignant irony of Danny dying in a school gang shooting. The film is carefully edited to present haunting echoes of words and scenes and the audience is left understanding that the pain of shame is universal (Lewis 1971). Derek's earlier words about the police rushing to the assistance of someone they love are echoed in the film's climax as we see Derek crying over his dead brother. We are left with the hope that Derek might better understand the consequences of burying his shame and that he might actually process his brother's death in a different, healthier way from how he responded to his father's.

We do not talk about shame enough but it is everywhere, in all of us, in all our families and our communities. We must experience our own shame and learn to process and tolerate the discomfort of it or risk continuing a generational cycle of violence and trauma. These are the same ideologies which can be heard in the world today and our insistence in clinging to certain beliefs, though they may feel culturally important and part of our identity, is directly responsible for perpetuating systems of shame and abuse that do not belong to one family alone. The shame of genocide is a shame that stains the world and belongs to us all.

Exercises

1. Think back to a time you might have attacked the other or attacked yourself. Can you locate the feeling of shame associated with that experience and how you might not have wanted to feel it?
2. Think back to a time you might have avoided or withdrawn. Can you locate the feeling of shame associated with that experience and how you might not have wanted to feel it?
3. The next time you feel shame, rather than choosing a point on the compass, what could you do differently?

References

Lewis, H.B. (1971). Shame and guilt in neurosis. *Psychoanalytic Review; New York.* 58 (3): 419–438.

Nathanson, D.L. (1992). *Shame and Pride: Affect, Sex, and the Birth of the Self.* New York: Norton.

Tomkins, S.S. (1991). *Affect/Imagery/Consciousness. Vol. 3: The Negative Affects: Anger and Fear.* New York: Springer.

20

Resilience and *The Omen*

Theory: Resilience

The psychological theory that regardless of the nature of our struggles in life, it is how we process them and what we do next that enable us to build resilience; to get back up when we fall down and continue to live a meaningful life.

Movie: *The Omen (1976)*

In a hospital in Rome where his wife has just given birth, an American diplomat, Robert Thorn, is told by the catholic priests that their son is stillborn. The priests encourage him to adopt a baby whose mother has died in childbirth that very night. Robert agrees, and Kathy believes the new baby to be her biological son, Damien. When Damien is an infant, his nanny hangs herself. A concerned member of the church, Father Brennan, starts to follow Robert, attempting to convince him that Damien is the Antichrist and trying to build an empire on earth using Robert's political power and business to legitimise his agenda. As people continue to die in bizarre and less and less coincidental circumstances, Robert starts to wonder if the prophecy is true and if something dark and dangerous does indeed now exist within his family.

What We're Doing?

In this chapter, we will be looking at the psychological theory of resilience in the movie, *The Omen*. As we learn about resilience, we will use it to understand and explore how all challenges in life offer us an opportunity to build resilience. Using my own experience in training, I invite you to consider how the theory may relate to your life.

A sunny day in September, sometime before lunch, I'm hit by the faint waft of coffee being made. I mention lunch to denote time rather than to imply I could have eaten a thing – my exam is imminent and I am so sickly nervous. I make sure there is no one in the house, no interruptions. It is just after the 2020 Covid-19 lockdown and the exam is being held online. It has been four long years, lots of money and no less tears, and now I wait alone, on a stool at the island in my kitchen, surrounded by what could be the set of the 2000 Christopher Nolan movie *Memento* – Post-its and posters full of different coloured notes plastered all over my cupboards to help me remember. Every inch of space taken up with quotes and definitions, authors and dates, anything and everything to help lodge into my brain what I already know but am scared I will forget. What if the doorbell rings? I won't answer, I think, and eventually they'll go away. This theory is tested when the postman rings ten minutes in, continuing to long press the bell and then for good measure adding a persistent knocking until he finally discovers the impetus to shove the package through the letterbox and I feel my whole body relax – a little.

An hour and ten minutes later, I hear the words '*You've passed Anoushka.*' I smile and then scream. The four examiners who have, from four small boxes on my laptop screen, examined my psychotherapeutic potential and given me their permission to call myself a psychotherapist, are beaming just like me – and then disappear. Poof. The screen goes dark, literally - the screen saver is a black night sky with only a few random stars left to illuminate the dark universe - and somewhere in the middle of that universe, I am now a qualified psychotherapist. Also, a Certified Transactional Analyst. Woo hoo. Applause? Party poppers? Hmmm. It's a little quiet in my kitchen. Did I miss the standing ovation?

I sit in the quiet of my success. I am aware that the first feeling I 'should be' experiencing at this moment is joy, a feeling that is conspicuous in its absence. It was less that joy had left the building and more that she had never entered. There were other emotions, all gathered in my kitchen – some standing, some leaning up against the counter, some sitting, slouched right beside me, but all present and most definitely accounted for. I took a moment to acknowledge sitting with them, this group, my feelings. They wore personalised sweatshirts so it was not hard to identify them. There was sadness – she was there to represent the sadness that my birth family were not, for a multitude of reasons, able to share in this moment. There was thoughtfulness, about my journey over the last four years and the cacophony of highs and lows. So much had happened and I saw a montage of all the experiences that the last four years of my life had brought. There was thankfulness, a feeling I did not expect to feel, who showed up to acknowledge all the difficult times, the lows that seemed like they would never end but that had, in their infinite wisdom, allowed me to grow and arrive at the point I found myself at now. There was pride – I was proud of myself, of who I had become and who I had shown myself to be to the four examiners who had met me for the first time and seen and accepted the me that was here today. And slightly away from the others, seated comfortably, albeit looking distantly out onto the lawn, was loneliness. She felt as strangely familiar as she did liberating. A kind of 'no going back,' this is where we were and the sobering realisation that though I had arrived here, I was still nowhere. I was reminded of a parable I heard once, maybe you know it, about the man who climbs as high as he can, achieving and scaling the heights of life until eventually he is there at the top, the highest point with nowhere else to go and he looks down and says, '*Is this it?*'

The surprise guest of honour though was resilience. She wore a tiara. She had found a way to be invited when it had felt impossible. The involuntary position of allowing yourself to collapse and going on to make the conscious decision that your life does matter. That you matter. The greatest losses and hardships we encounter are often the moments in life from which we build this resilience, sometimes for the first time. Depending on the circumstances, the resilience required will be different for everyone. At the time of writing this book, the world worries about Ukraine and the Middle East and asks when all the suffering will end. And that is just the suffering that we hear about.

It was in this awareness of my resilience through the course of my life and the serenity which had come from all of my different feelings being together in one room that the doorbell rang. It was not the postman this time, it was joy. '*Hello,*' she said, smiling, '*it felt like an important occasion. I was in the neighbourhood.*'

Growing up, *The Omen* was one of my favourite movies. It brought me so much healing and relief but above all, it brought me joy. It was the creative inspiration for so many directors and contains within it three of the best hanging, impaling and decapitation scenes in cinematic history, in that order. When we watch movies, we can have many emotional and visceral reactions. '*Ugh, she was so annoying,*' we might think about a character. The repulsion seems obvious but we might not be recognising this feeling in ourselves and the annoying parts of our own character in our own life. Rejecting the behaviour of a character allows us to elicit a strong reaction. Or we might say, '*She was crazy confident,*' about another character. Here, we have found a quality which we might relate to, or which we might even covet, wishing we could be more like that character. This is the power of movies: we can step out of our reality whilst simultaneously learning about our reality. The horror genre allows us to get a close-up yet safe look at aspects of life that we find scary or uncomfortable. To get up close and personal with fear and disgust and the parts of ourselves and others which we find fearful and disgusting. We are able to feel this fear safely and know that it can also leave us safely when the movie is over. We are left with the joy of feeling like we experienced fear without being left powerless, emotionally or physically hurt or left for dead. It also allows us to express our anger. There was nothing like a shocking and sudden decapitation to ease my after-school pain of being bullied. No other genre requires our resilience more to help survive the terror of the unthinkable. The fantasy of horror movies is rather like a dream state. In our dreams, we are given opportunities to shapeshift and to time travel as the conventional rules of form, structure and time do not apply to our unconscious. The people and objects in our dreams often represent aspects of ourselves or others around us. In this way, we can use *The Omen* and its illustration of multiple psychological concepts by imagining ourselves as exhibiting traits of all the characters rather than attaching ourselves to one character or one moral virtue that fits who we think we are or should be. So in this chapter, sit back and enjoy a psychological analysis of *The Omen* whilst you ponder on your own capacity for resilience.

'*The child is dead,*' are the first words of the film. We hear these words and immediately we are allowed to imagine the unthinkable: the death of a child. We are given permission. Permission in therapy is about helping the client feel empowered to give themselves permission. Permission for what? For whatever feels impossible. For whatever feels hard to say or do. **Where are you lacking permission in your life?**

These words also speak to the different parts of our psyche. Throughout our life, we can discover parts that are so neglected, forgotten or rejected they feel dead inside. Our sexual self, our creative self, our playful, joyous self. **What are the parts of you that feel dead inside? Do you have a relationship with your inner child?**

Robert Thorn rushes through the nighttime traffic of Rome in a taxi to be at the bedside of his wife, Kathy, who is giving birth. The priest informs him the baby is stillborn. '*I'm afraid it will kill her. She wanted a baby so much. What can I tell her?*' Immediately, the truth is seen as something so dangerous it could be fatal. Robert is told of a death and immediately predicts another. Robert catastrophises, he lies to Kathy and brings her a baby whose mother, he is told, died the same night. Robert places Kathy in the victim position on the drama triangle (Chapter 6) and positions himself as the rescuer, discounting her ability to cope, to grieve, to develop resilience as he offers a baby who, in truth, is not hers and who ironically does end up killing her.

How do we prevent the growth of those we love by telling ourselves the truth is too difficult for them to cope with?

Robert is appointed to the prestigious role of Ambassador to Great Britain and they move to England. Concordant classical music plays as the Thorns move into a beautiful new house with their son, Damien, now five years old. Watching their nanny, Holly, at Damien's birthday party, Kathy senses something is not right and tells Holly that she will take Damien. Even though Kathy is not Damien's real mother, she displays a mother's instinct that comes from her Nurturing Parent and is as powerful as one that is biological.

What is the true nature of your mother rather than the fantasy of 'the mother' and what purpose might the fantasy hold?

Surveying the lavish five-year-old's birthday party a photographer, Jennings, makes a comment about Damien's future – whether as '*heir to the Thorn fortune or the future Jesus Christ himself,*' a prophetic nod to Damien's antithetical identity and how we can hide parts of ourselves in plain sight. Holly, Damien's nanny, locks eyes with a rottweiler and discordant music – a synthesised rapid heartbeat – foretells something ominous. We hear Holly calling Damien's name and when the camera pans to her, she is standing precariously on the edge of the roof. '*It's all for you,*' Holly smiles as she jumps, a rope tightening around her neck as she shatters the glass of the window and swings right through it. Children scream and Kathy's eyes open wide and aghast in horror. This scene of pure noise is followed by one of eerie silence disrupted by the click of Jennings's camera. Director Richard Donner delights in contrasts, noise and silence, good and evil. Damien is clutched tightly in his parents' arms while his attention, like Holly's, is held by the rottweiler. Protection and punishment. The pulsing, throbbing synthesised beat returns as Damien waves at the beast. An idyllic family celebration has been grotesquely inverted. The perfect family is vulnerable; fantasy and reality at odds.

What image of perfection/goodness might be important to you in your life right now and, by upholding such a fantasy what might you be trying to ignore?

Father Brennan arrives to see Robert. '*We haven't much time,*' he says. Robert does not know this man and has never seen a priest more worried or harassed. Father Brennan starts to speak in rambling parables and warnings, '*I saw its mother.*' He demands that Robert '*accept Christ, drink his blood.*' The movie is an amalgamation of traditional Christian practice and symbolism as well as Satanic ritual and apocalypticism. Religion is often sought out for reasons of faith but it can also bring comfort, allaying the fears of an uncertain world. When religion becomes fused with fear and judgment, it creates a powerful inner conflict for the individual. **What is your relationship to religion? Do fear and judgment hold you back?**

As Father Brennan is thrown out of Robert's office, Jennings stands on the street, clicking his camera. In his dark room, he develops the photos from the birthday party as well as these of Father Brennan, and notices a strange red line near the nanny's head as well as the priest's.

Mrs. Baylock arrives at the Thorn family residence, announcing herself as Damien's new governess. Robert and Kathy are confused as they did not hire one. She tells the couple that the agency sent her after what happened to the old nanny. Alone with Damien, Mrs. Baylock reveals her sinister agenda as a demonic entity sent to protect Damien. On the morning of a family friend's wedding, Mrs. Baylock expresses her opinion that Damien is too young to understand a service at an episcopal church and should not be accompanying his parents. The Thorns ignore her but as they approach the church, Damien begins to get scared. **Can you remember moments in your life when a part of you did not want to do something but you conformed because of expectation? How did your physical body respond when your emotional body sent a different message?**

Damien is shaking and hides in his mother's arms. As the fear builds, he starts to scream. In a last-ditch attempt to stay away from the church, he pulls Kathy's hair and claws at her face. Kathy and Robert do not enter the church and return home instead. Robert asks if he should call a doctor, to which Kathy responds, *'they're just bruises.'* Robert confesses that he actually means a doctor for Damien. He says it's strange that Damien has never once fallen ill but Kathy insists they have nothing to worry about. Kathy refuses to consider how unusual it is for a five-year-old child to be so insusceptible. She fears the idea that Damien might not be 'normal.' **What is happening in your life that you are denying to yourself or to others? What might you be normalising that you should not be?**

Kathy worries about what Robert will think of her. He assures her that he loves her. Kathy's fear of how Robert will perceive her is a metaphor for how we view anything which does not fit within the 'norm' of society. Kathy's reaction to her fear is indicative of our own self-judgment towards the parts of ourselves that feel unacceptable. Little does she know that her fear is real, what with her son being the Antichrist. **What is your honest opinion regarding mental health and talking to a therapist and do you judge yourself or indeed others?**

Father Brennan finds Robert at a rugby match and warns him that his life is in danger. We see the same strange mark as before through Jennings' pictures. Brennan tells Robert about an old man called Bugenhagen, who Robert must meet in the town of Megiddo in the old city of Jezreel. Bugenhagen warns of the devil in human form and forewarns that Kathy is pregnant but that Damien will not let another child of theirs live. Brennan tells him that Damien will kill Kathy, and then Robert, '*establishing his counterfeit kingdom on Earth*,' taking orders from the devil himself.

Where might you self-sabotage and allow your Critical Parent voice to dominate and instruct you?

The wind whips into a frenzy and a storm ensues. Brennan seeks shelter from the elements as clouds cluster in the sky. Lightning strikes, a branch catches alight, snaps and falls to the ground amidst sinister Latin chanting. Brennan tries to enter the church but cannot open the door. Thunder roars and a metal spire falls from the roof and impales Brennan straight through his body, pinning him upright, dead in the ground. The storm breaks and the sun emerges.

Are you ignoring the signs that there is a part of you that needs to meta-phorically die before the sun – the new you – can come out?

When Robert arrives home after meeting Brennan, Kathy tells him she is pregnant and wants an abortion. Her doctor tells Robert about Kathy's 'fantasies,' that her son is not hers. The doctor says having another child now would be a mistake because Kathy's mental state is too fragile. Therapeutically, the doctor is saying that before Kathy can take care of another, she must be able to take care of herself. Kathy's intuition is correct, but Robert is adamant that the unborn baby must not die. His refusal to see the reality of what is happening puts them both in danger.

Where in your life do you not trust your higher self or your gut instinct and allow yourself to be overruled?

A maniacal Damien rides his tricycle up and down the narrow upstairs corridor. Mrs. Baylock sees the opportunity and opens a door to allow Damien access. Riding out onto the first-floor balcony, Damien knocks Kathy off a stool on which she is standing to water a plant. She topples headfirst over the bannister, breaking a goldfish bowl and falling to the floor. She lies unconscious surrounded by shattered glass, spilt water and slow flapping fish, blood dripping. When Robert arrives at the hospital he hears she has lost the baby. The doctor does not know that this was attempted murder and offers Robert all the reasons he should be grateful his wife is okay.

Do you or anyone around you engage in toxic positivity to avoid feeling uncomfortable feelings?

Kathy begs Robert, '*don't let him kill me.*' Jennings shows him the red line that appears over everyone connected to Robert, all now either dead or in danger, including Jennings himself. Robert and Jennings travel to Rome for answers. The hospital where Kathy and Robert were given Damien burned down in a fire five years ago, just after Damien's birth. The priest that handed Damien to Robert is now in a secluded monastery after being burned in the fire, his sight and speech damaged. They are told he has abandoned Christ and diverted off the expected path.

When have you needed to find a new path in life?

Father Brennan has a 666 birthmark and Robert is told Damien must have it too. The 666 denotes the devil, the Antichrist and the false prophet, which mirrors the Christian holy trinity of the father, son and holy ghost – as well as the transactional analysis trinity of Parent, Adult and Child. '*For everything holy there is something unholy,*' is an important line in the film, signifying the theory of spiritual opposites.

In psychology, opposites begin with the ego and the shadow. Carl Jung (1974) coined the term 'enantiodromia' as the psychological arrival of what is unconsciously opposite to what is consciously demonstrated. Robert's career and the Thorn family fortune are firmly entrenched in the materialistic world. Kathy's exterior image is described by Robert as '*too sexy for the White House,*' demonstrating the couple's outward perception and focus. But there is also a fear of what is imperfect and unknown, a lack of control relegated to the shadows. The horror of the imperfect child. Raising the devil incarnate has meant the couple have had to embark on sudden and inward-turning journeys, more spiritually driven, where they are forced to strip away their outward masks.

What aspect of you lies buried in the shadows or behind a mask?

Jennings and Robert discover that the priest had lied all those years ago in the hospital and that Robert and Kathy's biological child was murdered at birth and buried in a wild cemetery in Rome. They also learn that Damien's real mother was a jackal buried in a tomb next to Robert's dead biological son. Robert can no longer avoid the truth. He calls Kathy and begs her to leave the country as soon as possible. As Kathy hangs up the phone, Mrs. Baylock arrives and pushes her from the hospital window to her death. Robert's world is turned upside down and he plunges into grief, experiencing some of its aspects: shock, denial, sadness and anger.

When has your world become unrecognisable through loss?

Bugenhagen impresses upon Robert that Damien is not a human child and that this human form Satan has assumed must be stabbed with special holy knives. Robert takes the knives but has a change of heart. Jennings says he will do what needs to be done if Robert cannot find the courage but a pane of glass inexplicably slides off a mysteriously reversing vehicle and Jennings is decapitated.

What has required unimaginable courage in your life?

Mrs Baylock tries to kill Robert. He manages to save himself but is shot and killed by the police before he can do the unthinkable and kill Damien. At Robert and Kathy's funeral, Damien holds the hand of the President of the United States and, in a nod to the transference of power, Damien turns around and smiles sweetly at the audience.

How is generational trauma passed down in your family?

Exercises

1. Looking back on your life, what is your relationship to resilience?
2. Who and what brings you joy in your life today?
3. In the movie of your life how do the characters resilience and joy get along?

Reference

Jung, C.G. (1974). *Psychological Types* (The Collected Works of CG Jung, Vol. 6). Princeton, NJ: Princeton University Press.

Epilogue

All I know is this: nobody's very big in the first place, and it looks to me like everybody spends their whole life tearing everybody else down.
Randle P. McMurphy – *One Flew Over the Cuckoo's Nest*

There are so many more films and theories that I would have loved to have written about. I cannot imagine a world without film, I do not want to. These films encapsulate the human experience, which often feels an impossible one. The films in this book, and indeed the theories I have chosen, have meant something to me at different times in my life, and still do. Psychotherapeutic work is not an easy path. Looking at our shadow self, the parts of ourselves we do not like very much and make us feel uncomfortable, is painful. Films (not to mention outstanding television series) have been constant and healing companions in this shadow work. And no matter the theory or the film, I notice the sense of shame and the experience of loss were somewhere inside every chapter. How does this shame and loss find us? What is within our control and what is not? Human beings are incredibly skilled at not only inflicting pain but also enduring it and we choose to use our physical and emotional bodies to wield an attack or to bear one. The world we live in is a reflection of how we use our physical and emotional bodies, and we now understand more about trauma and the fact that unprocessed emotion is passed through the blood to the baby and into the next generation. There are biological facts behind the often-colloquially used expression, 'it's in my blood.'

The human experience is, up to this point at least, characterised by shame and loss. A particularly poignant experience of loss is the loss of family, a pain which is quickly followed by the shame of what we cannot bear and what we fail to comprehend. This book was conceived and written, with love, in the hope of helping to better understand who we are underneath all the layers of 'stuff' that we carry. The characters in films are flawed and vulnerable, and that is why we can relate to them. They give us permission to look at the parts of ourselves that are flawed and vulnerable. They start off hating each other and in less than two hours are best friends. We are moved by the idea of reconciliation in a world where difference is so threatening. Movies can help us understand something about difference and allow a slow fade up from the shadows, panning to a softer and more compassionate focus on us as the main character.

Aside from being a slang term for an insane asylum, the cuckoo's nest is somewhat of a misnomer. The cuckoo actually lays its egg in the nests of other birds – behaviour known as brood parasitism – who go on to raise the little chick as one of their own. Families play a significant role in the growth and development of humans but, when you feel like the cuckoo, the other people in the nest can seem like a different species. Thank you, with so much love, to the two birds who crossed the water and built the nest I grew up in, and to the other little chick for sitting in it with me for as long as we did.

It is in the hope that, by living a more conscious life where we can love ourselves with more honesty, we can lessen the pain of shame and of loss and perhaps make living a life a little easier. I have the utmost admiration for all those who embark on the journey of return to the self.

Index

Printed and bound by CPI Group (UK) Ltd, Croydon, CR0 4YY

10/05/2026

14875867-0001